Ovid Unseens

Other Latin Language Learning titles from Bloomsbury

Latin Unseens for A Level, Ashley Carter
9781853996818

Latin Beyond GCSE, John Taylor
9781853997204

Writing Latin, James Morwood and Richard Ashdowne
9781853997013

Advanced Latin: Materials for A2 and PRE-U, James Morwood,
Katharine Radice and Stephen Anderson
9781853997297

Ovid Unseens

Practice Passages for Latin Verse Translation and Comprehension

Mathew Owen

B L O O M S B U R Y

LONDON · NEW DELHI · NEW YORK · SYDNEY

Bloomsbury Academic

An imprint of Bloomsbury Publishing Plc

50 Bedford Square   1385 Broadway
London   New York
WC1B 3DP   NY 10018
UK   USA

www.bloomsbury.com

Bloomsbury is a registered trademark of Bloomsbury Publishing Plc

First published 2014

© Mathew Owen, 2014

British Library Cataloguing-in-Publication Data
A catalogue record for this book is available from the British Library.

ISBN: PB: 978-1-4725-0984-0
ePub: 978-1-4725-0787-7
ePDF: 978-1-4725-1241-3

Library of Congress Cataloging-in-Publication Data
A catalog record for this book is available from the Library of Congress.

Typeset by Refinecatch Limited, Bungay, Suffolk

Contents

Preface

This book's genesis was as a collection of passages for sixth formers at Caterham to practise the Ovid unseen, which is one of the A2 Latin examination's most challenging elements. It is intended primarily, therefore, for those preparing for A2, and certain aspects of the book are tailored specifically to these examinations.

The book comprises two halves which work independently of one another. The first forty passages are drawn from Ovid's elegiac poetry, the second from the *Metamorphoses*. This is to cater for the rotation of prescribed unseen material between elegiac and hexameter verse.

Within each forty-passage half, the passages are roughly graduated in terms of syntax and vocabulary to build the student's confidence when presented with a passage of Ovid's poetry. There is not, however, a perfect curve, mainly owing to the indefinibility of 'difficulty': any teacher knows that what one student seems to find very straightforward, another will struggle with. Passages 1–20 in each half are shorter passages for translation only, and 21–40 are longer, with questions on comprehension, stylistic analysis and scansion.

The introduction to each passage is given in a uniform way: first, an overview of the content of the Latin passage; and then (in italics) a lead-in, paraphrasing the lines immediately before the passage itself begins.

At the back of the book is a vocabulary list of 450 words which are either distinctively Ovidian or which, though equally common in prose, feature regularly in Ovid's poetry. It has inevitably been impossible to pitch this perfectly for the needs of all, but most of the words included are not only likely to be new to first-time readers of Ovid but are also among the most commonly recurring items of vocabulary in his poetry. A debt to John Taylor's verse vocabulary list in *Latin Beyond GCSE* (London: Bristol Classical Press, 2009) in compiling this one is freely admitted.

The vocabulary is grouped in checklists (1–10), each of about forty words and each corresponding to a group of four passages. These checklists cover **both** the elegiac **and** hexameter halves: so Checklist 1 contains the new words from Elegiac Passages 1–4 **and** Hexameter Passages 1–4. In this way, the whole vocabulary list is covered in a steady and cumulative manner, regardless of which half of the book is being used. There is also a list of Fifty Starter Verse Words, knowledge of which is assumed from the first passage onwards.

Words which are neither likely to be known nor appear in the vocabulary list are glossed below each passage. The later passages are glossed more sparingly, requiring students to deduce meaning of unfamiliar words to an increasing extent. Proper nouns are generally glossed, unless they appear in the vocabulary list or are obvious from the preamble to the passage.

The first fifteen passages in each half feature a *Discendum* box, in which a peculiarity of Latin verse is discussed. These are usually facets which experience indicates students struggle with, and which often seem to go unexplained. For some, these discussions may seem too basic, for others, too advanced, but it is hoped that they will at least be useful springboards for teachers and reminders for students.

Finally, the *Introduction to Scansion* aims to give a summary of the operation of Latin metre commensurate with the likely level of proficiency of this book's audience. The four steps cover most of what a beginner will need to know to be able to scan hexameters and pentameters accurately. Each step has a practice exercise, solutions for which can be found at the end of the book to allow students to practise independently.

While this book has been written with A2 students particularly in mind, it is hoped that others will also find it of use: those preparing for equivalent school examinations will be required to achieve similar levels of proficiency in unseen verse translation as A2 candidates; and the coverage of all of Ovid's major works in this collection would suit adult newcomers to Ovid or those preparing for university applications.

The kindness and generosity of the classical teaching profession has been remarkable and humbling, and in putting this book together I have incurred more debts than I can hope to repay: to John Taylor at Tonbridge and John Godwin at Shrewsbury; to my friend and colleague at Caterham, Kristian Waite; and to my own inspiring teachers, Sue Herbert, Llewelyn Morgan and Richard Smail, all of whom have given their time and encouragement liberally and unstintingly. Much of this book is theirs, but all mistakes are my own. Finally, I am immensely grateful to Charlotte Loveridge and Dhara Patel at Bloomsbury, who could not have been more supportive throughout this project.

Mathew Owen
Caterham School

Abbreviations

abl.	ablative	*indecl.*	indeclinable
acc.	accusative	*infin.*	infinitive
c.	common (*m./f.*)	*lit.*	literally
dat.	dative	*m.*	masculine
decl.	declension	*n.*	neuter
f.	feminine	*nom.*	nominative
gen.	genitive	*pl.*	plural
Gk	Greek	*sing.*	singular
impers.	impersonal	*voc.*	vocative

Am.	Amores	*Met.*	Metamorphoses
Ars Am.	Ars Amatoria	*Rem. Am.*	Remedia Amoris
Ex Ponto	Epistulae ex Ponto	*Tr.*	Tristia
Her.	Heroides		

Introduction to Ovid

Almost everything we know about Publius Ovidius Naso derives from his poems, where it is not always easy to distinguish genuine autobiographical fact from poetic persona. About certain details, however, we can be fairly confident. He was born in 43 BC in the town of Sulmo (modern Sulmona) in central Italy, about 130 km from Rome. His father was a member of the second tier of Rome's social hierarchy: he was a knight (*eques*), not a senator but a member of the landed gentry, a man of significant means. He was rich enough to educate Ovid and his elder brother in the traditional manner of the Roman élite, sending them to Rome to study law and rhetoric in preparation for careers as barristers and politicians.

But pursuit of the various magistracies of the Roman state (the so-called *cursus honorum*) clearly held no appeal for Ovid and, no doubt to his father's dismay, his focus quickly moved to literature and poetry. His talents here were spotted early: he tells us that, before he officially came of age, the literary patron Messalla Corvinus took an interest in his poetry and received him into his circle of litterateurs (*Ex Ponto* II.3.75), which included some of the greatest poets of the age. Ovid lists with pride (at *Tristia* IV.10.43ff.) the luminaries with whom he associated in his early career, and contact with these men must have had a very profound impact on a young man with poetic ambitions. He knew Tibullus, albeit briefly, he 'saw' Virgil (clearly overawed by the experience), and he developed relationships with Horace and Propertius.

Ovid had married for the first time when he was only about 16 years old. The union was evidently not a happy one (he later assessed his first wife rather savagely as 'unworthy and useless'), and seems to have been dissolved after only two years. At around the same time, Ovid's beloved brother died and, no doubt in part as a tonic, Ovid left Rome on a two-year tour of Greece and the East. On his return (c. 22 BC) he tells us he resumed, somewhat half-heartedly, the political career his father so desired for him, holding some very junior magistracies and administrative positions in Rome. These responsibilities, however, would have demanded little of his energies and he evidently found plenty of time to continue his literary endeavours in this period.

Ovid would have found in the Rome of the 20s BC not only a feeling of literary vibrancy among his artistic associates, but also a broader feeling of renovation and renewal. For Ovid had been born at a time of extraordinary crisis in the Roman republic. In the year before his birth, Julius Caesar, after five years of one-man rule, had been assassinated by his senatorial enemies; in the year Ovid was born, the great statesman and orator Cicero had been murdered and butchered by Mark Antony; and in 44–31 BC vicious and bloody civil wars had ripped the empire apart. It was the victory of Octavian at Actium in 31 BC which, at last, ended these wars and established a durable peace across the Roman world.

Octavian, taking the name Augustus, then embarked upon an ambitious programme to heal the wounds inflicted during generations of corruption, decline and internecine blood-letting. Styling himself the restorer of the republic, not emperor but 'first among equals', he revolutionized the Roman state to ensure stability and order. In addition, he set about transforming republican Rome's famously shabby appearance, finding, as he boasted, a city of mud-brick and leaving one of marble. But he also looked to revive all that he saw as most noble in the history of Rome, especially in the moral sphere. His social programme evoked the pristine purity of the good old days of the early republic, advocating a simple life of honesty and hard work and legislating to penalize adultery and childlessness.

Even if their works sometimes complicate and even subvert the emperor's ideology, many poets of the age are palpably sympathetic to the regime's programme. Virgil's great patriotic epic the *Aeneid* is, on one level at least, a hymn to Roman virtues of manliness, valour and devotion to duty; his *Georgics*, set in the world of the hardy farmer, encourage traditional and simple values; and Horace's *Odes* often brim with praise for the emperor and his revolution. Ovid, however, seems to have been constitutionally incapable of such seriousness and reverence. From the very outset, his poetry ran against the grain of Augustus' social programme, revelling in the tawdry, the sexy and the naughty and avoiding, even deriding, the grandeur of the project which Virgil, Horace and many of their peers were celebrating.

Amores

Ovid set out his stall in his first work, the *Amores* (*Love Affairs*), published in 16 BC (though the three-book edition which survives may well have been published rather later). The reader follows 'Ovid' through the ups and downs of his love-life, especially his relationship with a girl called Corinna with whom he is infatuated. We read of his steamy successes (I.5), his spectacular failures (III.7), his hopeful love letters, disappointing replies, days, nights, dreams and fears. Quite apart from the complex literary allusions and the elegance of the language, the *Amores* are an intensely engaging saga in which Ovid travels through the full gamut of love's emotions. The question of the reality of the stories or characters, especially that of Corinna, is too complex for this brief discussion. But while the scenery of the poems must have been founded in the Rome which Ovid inhabited, and while there are moments when we cannot fail to hear the voice of the real Ovid (his lament on Tibullus' death, III.9, for instance), it would be a mistake to read the *Amores* as autobiographical diaries. Corinna may have been based on an object of the poet's affections (he insists at *Tristia* IV.10.59 that she was), but in a sense it is scarcely important; she fills the role of the elegiac *domina* which was a staple of the genre, and provides a literary figure towards whom the emotions of the lover can be directed.

The *Amores'* subject matter and form were not entirely new but rather joined a tradition of personal love elegy which had flourished during the previous few decades in the poetry of Gallus, Propertius and Tibullus. Nor indeed, despite some very intimate scenes ranging from passionate afternoons with Corinna through abortions to Ovid's sexual shortcomings, are they especially lewd by the standards of Roman poetry – certainly they fall well short of some of Catullus' more explicit material. They were, however, a new approach to the genre of elegy and often seem, if not to parody, at least to poke gentle fun by their engagement with the elegies of Ovid's contemporaries, reworking elegiac commonplaces with a tongue-in-cheek tone. They also seem in many instances to run very much against the grain of the values the emperor was trying to propagate. Against the backdrop of the *leges Iuliae* of 18 BC, which aimed to encourage marriage and punish adultery, Ovid's publication two years later of poems in which an adulterer laments the presence of his lover's husband at a dinner party (I.4), or a husband is encouraged to pimp out his wife (III.4), must have raised some eyebrows in the court of Augustus.

In more subtle ways, too, Ovid's *Amores* swim against the Augustan tide. As the emperor's *restitutio rei publicae* sought to shore up the social hierarchy, Ovid delights in depicting the (upper-class) lover as a slave to his mistress (e.g. II.17), trapped in the so-called *servitium amoris* (slavery of love). And while Augustus' propaganda appealed to the military glories of Rome and the warrior virtues of her citizens, Ovid, who seems himself to have avoided the military service a man of his station would usually have undertaken, is recasting love as a type of warfare with the bedroom as the battleground: the *militia amoris* (soldiery of love). The first word of the *Amores* is *arma* (weapons), not only a literary play on the identical first word of Virgil's heroic patriotic epic, the *Aeneid*, but also an early indication of the recurring martial imagery in Ovid's poetry. We can only imagine what a more serious-minded Augustan thought as he read of Cupid celebrating a triumph (I.2), a lover's empty threats that he will storm his sweetheart's house like a city (I.6) or Ovid's assertion that a lover is a gallant and hardy soldier (I.9).

Heroides

Despite (or perhaps because of) this, Ovid's *Amores* were a success and made his name as a poet. At about the same date, he produced a very different set of poems which picked up and developed the mythological material he had made regular, if rather playful, use of in the *Amores*. During his rhetorical training, the young Ovid would have become well acquainted with the *ethopoeia*, in which the student was given a scenario from ancient history or mythology and required to form a speech in character. Such exercises were surely part of Ovid's inspiration for his *Heroides* (Heroines), imagined letters in verse from mythological women to their heroic lovers, who have in some way hurt them. So Dido writes to Aeneas to complain of his sudden departure, and Ariadne to Theseus, telling of her grief at being abandoned on Naxos. *Heroides* I–XV are from women to their men (all mythical characters except XV, which is from the Greek poet Sappho); and then, in what are known as the 'Double *Heroides*', almost certainly released in later years, letters XVI–XXI are paired poems of both letter and reply.

The cocktail of elements from other genres (epic mythology, elegiac themes, epistolary form, rhetorical exercises, etc.) makes the *Heroides* unique in the corpus of extant ancient poetry. There is, as always, considerable humour in these poems, often stemming from deliberately clumsy anachronism. Moreover, in the *Heroides* Ovid effectively reverses what he had done with myth in the *Amores*: there, mundane and even sordid love was elevated to the grandeur of mythology, whereas in this collection, figures from the heroic past are presented with all the anxieties and foibles of contemporary everyday lovers. There are also moments of greater profundity, sadness and poignancy, and of course ubiquitous allusion to Ovid's literary forebears, both Greek and Roman. But what will strike the first-time reader above all in this collection is the centrality of the feminine, so rare and remarkable in a literary world in which the male voice was entirely dominant. We may, it is true, sometimes doubt that in his portrayal of the thoughts of heroines Ovid exhibits the mastery of female psychology with which he evidently believed himself endowed. Nevertheless, the letters of the *Heroides* constitute a most unusual, delightful and fascinating collection of poems.

Ars Amatoria

Ovid's next work survives only in a fragment. The *Medicamina Faciei Femineae* (*Facial Treatment for Ladies*) is an extraordinary poem, again in the elegiac metre, which gives make-up tips to his imagined female readership. And, although his recipes of lupin seeds and flatulence-inducing beans have largely fallen into disuse in modern cosmetics, the *Medicamina* represents Ovid's first experiment with the concept which would yield his two next, more celebrated poems.

'Didactic' or 'teaching' poetry was a genre with a long history, again stretching back to the Greek poets and culminating in Lucretius' great philosophical work *De Rerum Natura* and the *Georgics* of Virgil. Ovid's innovation, however, was didactic poetry whose themes were not the grand ones of philosophy, farming or citizenship but rather love, seduction and coquetry. And so, again, Ovid takes a long-established genre and makes it distinctively his own: the humorous tone and the amatory themes of the *Ars Amatoria* (*The Art of Love*) and the *Remedia Amoris* (*Cures for Love*) are without parallel in classical didactic literature.

We find in these works the poet's persona markedly changed from the *Amores*. Then he was the elegiac lover, ardent, desperate and always at the mercy of Cupid and his mistress; but now he is a canny *praeceptor amoris* (instructor of love) who teaches love-making as a cynical if light-hearted science. The first two books of the *Ars Amatoria* (published c. AD 1) claim to give instruction to his male readers on how to find girls, seduce them and make them their own. Mythological references abound (indeed, he begins the *Ars* by comparing himself to Achilles' tutor, Chiron, or Jason's helmsman, Tiphys) and are deployed for often bathetic effect: the myth of Orion is adduced as evidence that a lover should keep a pale complexion; of Odysseus that absence can make a heart grow fonder; of Theseus that men should not use hair-clips.

Book III of the *Ars* is written ostensibly for a female readership (though with the voyeuristic male reader always in mind) and in a tone similar to the *Medicamina* it instructs inexperienced young girls in the ways of love. Ovid's poetry is again full of wit and humour as he explains why he would have avoided Ajax and Hector's frigid wives in favour of a more tender lover, or exhorts girls to adopt the same hard-to-get tactics (III.581) which so frustrated the Ovid of the *Amores* (I.6). A lurid catalogue of sexual positions constitutes a fitting climax to a poem which parodies both the didactic genre and the theme of love in poetry more widely, including Ovid's own.

Remedia Amoris

In the same year as the *Ars Amatoria* (c. AD 1) Ovid published its
antidote, the *Remedia Amoris*. This time the poet is a doctor or
counsellor, offering advice, predominantly to young men, concerning
how to avoid becoming besotted with a girl, how to break off affairs,
and how to deal with the end of relationships. It is as flippant and as
delightful as the *Ars*, with the same humorous look at love and lovers
and the same Ovidian irreverence. The very act of publishing two
purportedly didactic poems arguing opposite positions in the same
year tells its own story.

But these two works, evoking the frivolity and loose morals of
Rome's élite society, were unfortunately timed. In 2 BC, Augustus'
infamous daughter Julia was exiled to the island of Pandataria for a
string of alleged liaisons with young noblemen in or around the
Augustan court. This was profoundly damaging for the emperor: he
had not only framed laws to combat adultery (the *lex Iulia de adulteriis
coercendis* of 18 BC) but had also held up the imperial family as the
model of a healthy Roman family, depicted (Julia included) on the
great Altar of Peace he had constructed in the heart of the city. And so,
whatever the popularity of the *Ars Amatoria* and the *Remedia Amoris*
in Rome, we can be sure that the emperor received them with little
enthusiasm.

Metamorphoses

Perhaps aware of this, Ovid's poetry after AD 1 takes a sharp turn away
from the themes of love and daily (or nightly) life which dominated
his early career. In the years leading up to AD 8, Ovid composed the
15-book *Metamorphoses* (*Changes of Shape*), his first and only work in
the epic metre of dactylic hexameters. And the scope of the poem is

certainly epic: it takes as its starting point the birth of the universe from primordial chaos and ends with the deification of Julius Caesar and Augustus. Its setting, too, is far from the salons and back streets of Rome, in the world of myths, heroes and gods. As for length, Ovid outdoes even the great Virgil himself, whose 12-book *Aeneid*, just two decades after its publication, was already the definitive Latin epic.

One of epic's definitive features, however, is unity of plot, a narrative which plays out over the course of the poem. In this regard, the *Metamorphoses* is decidedly un-epic: although the hundreds of little tales which constitute the poem are skilfully and elegantly woven into one another, it is certainly not a continuum. Likewise, the tales which make up the poem arise in myriad contexts, sometimes told by the narrator, sometimes by a character. Ovid in the *Metamorphoses* marries the scale of traditional epic with the devotion to shortness, the 'slender Muse', of Ovid's Hellenistic forebears, and all bound by the unifying thread of metamorphosis. Perhaps this theme extends to the genre of the poem itself, which continues to elude easy categorization.

As might be expected, the tone of the poem is markedly different from that of his erotic poetry. Nevertheless, albeit in a more subtle way, Ovid is as impish and irreverent as ever. He has characters within his own stories mock the idea of metamorphosis as made-up nonsense (VIII.614); he presents Jupiter, king of the gods, as a seedy rapist from the very start of the poem, taking Io's virginity on a whim in a dark wood; and then, at the poem's culmination, he equates Augustus with Jupiter in a panegyric which leaves it suggestively ambiguous whether we are to imagine Jupiter enthroned in majesty or as the rather oversexed and very human character which the preceding 15 books have introduced.

The *Metamorphoses* encompasses an enormous range of stories and has become something of a handbook of Greek and Roman mythology. The individual tales also vary greatly, from those of obvious transformation (Daphne becomes a tree, Actaeon a stag, etc.)

to less literal changes of form (Daedalus and Icarus are not actually turned into birds) to tales where there seems no real metamorphosis at all (such as the tale of Proserpina). But they all exhibit Ovid's poetic virtuosity and genius at its zenith, drawing the reader to suspend his disbelief and to delight in the magical world the poet creates.

Fasti

Composed at the same time as the *Metamorphoses* were the six books of the *Fasti* (*Calendar*) which survive. They take as their subject the world of ancient history and mythological pre-history, delving into Rome's past to explain traditions and curiosities in her contemporary calendar. The *Fasti*, however, does not trace the story of the universe in a linear progression or follow any particular theme through time, but instead gives the origins of specifically Roman festal days in calendrical rather than chronological order. Thus the mythical story of Arion and the Dolphin can be followed immediately by mention of Romulus and Remus and Augustus himself.

The *Fasti's* inspirations seem manifold. Julius Caesar's reform of the Roman calendar a few decades before, in 45 BC, perhaps provided the opportunity for a poetic exploration of some important Roman dates. But there is a literary inspiration as well: the *Fasti*, explaining as it does the origins of customs and practices in short episodes, has as its antecedent one of the most celebrated poems of the Alexandrian era, Callimachus' *Aetia* (*Origins*). Finally there is a degree to which Ovid is tapping into a contemporary vogue for antiquarianism, led from the front by Augustus in his attempts to found his new regime in the religious and cultural traditions of the Roman republic.

Yet Ovid's poem is again *sui generis*. For a start, there is the tension between the grand national and religious subject matter and the more intimate elegiac metre and tone, which enables the poet to make a personal journey through the peculiarities of the calendar. It is not a dry history but rather full of Ovid's characteristic variety; in the persona of an interested but not terribly knowledgeable historian, he asks gods and heroes for explanations and back-stories as he journeys to the corners of the Roman world and beyond. Naturally, there are moments of wit as well, such as Venus' nod and wink to Ovid at the opening of Book IV as she wonders to see the man who penned the *Amores* and the *Ars* busy about an aetiological study of Roman feast days.

Exile

The *Fasti*'s six books stop short of the two Julian months, July and August (named in honour of Julius Caesar and Augustus respectively). We cannot tell whether this was a deliberate snub by Ovid, or whether the emperor bundled him out of the city before he could turn his satirical gaze on these months. Whatever the truth of the matter, in the year AD 8 Augustus banished Ovid from Rome.

By this time, with Virgil, Tibullus, Propertius and Horace all dead, Ovid was indisputably the pre-eminent literary figure in Rome; he had been happily married to his third wife for several years; and his recent poetry, the *Metamorphoses* and the *Fasti*, had steered clear of the more risqué themes of his earlier career. In this context, his *relegatio* (exile without loss of property or citizenship) to the Black Sea coast by an angry emperor seems baffling.

Indeed, the precise cause of Ovid's exile remains one of the most abiding and insoluble mysteries in the history of literature. He himself talks of *carmen et error* (a poem and a mistake). The *Ars Amatoria* can confidently be taken to be the identity of the former: both its salacious tone, running counter to Augustus' censorious tendencies, and its timing in the immediate aftermath of Julia's banishment, made it potentially highly dangerous. As for the *error*, centuries of speculation have left us still very much in the dark. It seems likely, however, that Ovid saw something he ought not to have seen. This may well have been connected to the sexual improprieties of Julia which had earned her exile. Or it is possible that Ovid overheard details of the conspiracy, discovered in 2 BC, to take the reins of the empire after Augustus' death, led by aristocratic young men around Julia who would have moved in Ovid's circles. Indeed, there is every chance that the exile of the emperor's daughter Julia in 2 BC and of her own daughter (also Julia) in AD 8, Ovid's banishment and the censoring of the *Ars* were all designed by the regime to paint what had been a political crisis or even an attempted coup as a mere sexual scandal.

Tristia and *Epistulae ex Ponto*

Whatever the exact cause, with his *Metamorphoses* not quite fully polished and his *Fasti* half done, Ovid left Rome in the winter of AD 8, never to return. And Augustus had chosen his place of exile with vindictive ingenuity. Tomis (modern Constanța in Romania) on the coast of the Black Sea could not have been further removed from the refined world Ovid had inhabited in Rome. Gone was the circle of young artists admiringly fawning on him, gone the wine and wit of the dinner parties in the homes of the rich and powerful, gone the libraries, the Latin speakers, the urbane friends, even his own wife and family. The misery Ovid records in his poems from exile could scarcely have been more exquisite.

Naturally, Ovid's poetry was changed by his banishment. The five books of his *Tristia* (*Sorrows*) and four of his *Epistulae ex Ponto* (*Letters from the Black Sea*) have been described by one critic as 'communication from the tomb' (Hardie, 2000, p.152). They are again in the elegiac metre, whose Greek origins were in 'elegies' or laments, and in them

Ovid bewails every facet of his life in Tomis. Like the locked-out lover of the *Amores*, Ovid is kept from everything he most loves in Rome. Sometimes he hopes for a reprieve, addressing Augustus himself and begging forgiveness; at other times he remembers Rome like a previous life, vanished forever; and throughout he paints a graphic and highly exaggerated picture of the horrors of the land he now inhabits, where bandits' arrows fly through the streets and such is the cold that wine is not drunk but eaten in frozen chunks.

Although a modern audience might weary of his complaints, Ovid's exile poetry is far from dull. There are moments of profound pathos as he remembers the morning he left his wife and home forever, touching tributes to loyal friends and even glimpses of wit and levity. But if Ovid ever really hoped that these poems would win him an imperial pardon, he was to be disappointed. He was, as he put it, 'blasted by Jupiter's thunderbolt' and neither Augustus nor his successor Tiberius ever recalled Ovid to Rome. And so it was that, far from his beloved wife and city, on the margins of the Roman world, Ovid died in AD 17.

Legacy

Ovid has a strong claim to be the most influential of all Roman poets on the evolution of western literature. Every age has found something to delight it in his corpus, and so his popularity has been perennial. His poetry, especially the *Metamorphoses*, was taught in schools and universities across Europe during the Middle Ages, and Chaucer's *Canterbury Tales* reveal Ovidian influence in both form and content. Later, a translation of Ovid was one of the first works to emerge from Caxton's printing press. It is also certain that Shakespeare had some considerable knowledge of Ovid: poems such as *Venus and Adonis*, plays such as *Titus Andronicus* and moments such as the famous 'play

within a play' of Pyramus and Thisbe in *A Midsummer Night's Dream*
betray the unmistakable presence of Ovid, about whom Shakespeare
himself wrote, 'for elegance, facility and golden cadence of poesy . . .
Ovidius Naso was the man' (*Love's Labours Lost*, IV.2). If Virgil was the
dominant poetic influence on Milton, Ovid was his favourite reading.
And such devotion to his work has not abated in the centuries leading
to the modern era, where T. S. Eliot, James Joyce and, most recently,
Ted Hughes have left their debt to Ovid in no doubt. Hughes's
wonderful renderings of passages of the *Metamorphoses* in *Tales
from Ovid* has put Ovid back at the centre of the modern literary
consciousness and would be an especially rewarding read for those
about to begin translating Ovid themselves.

Further Reading

The Penguin Classics translations of Ovid's poetry and their
introductions are a highly recommended starting point for further
exploration, as are:

Armstrong, R. (2005) *Ovid and his Love Poetry*, London: Duckworth.

Brown, S. A. (2005) *Ovid: Myth and Metamorphosis*, Bristol: Bristol Classical
Press.

Butler, C. (2011) 'Ovid', in Croally, N. and Hyde, R. (eds) *Classical Literature:
An Introduction*, London and New York: Routledge, pp.296–304.

Fantham, E. (2004) *Ovid's Metamorphoses*, Oxford: Oxford University Press.

Galinsky, G. K. (1975) *Ovid's Metamorphoses: An Introduction to the Basic
Aspects*, Oxford: Blackwell.

Hardie, P. (2000) 'Coming to terms with the Empire: poetry of the later
Augustan and Tiberian period', in Taplin, O. (ed.) *Literature in the Roman
World*, Oxford: Oxford University Press, pp.119–53.

Hardie, P. (ed.) (2002) *The Cambridge Companion to Ovid*, Cambridge:
Cambridge University Press.

Holzberg, N. (2002) *Ovid: the Poet and his Work*, Ithaca: Cornell University Press.

Hughes, T. (1997) *Tales from Ovid*, London: Faber and Faber.

Kenney, E. J. (1982) 'Ovid', in Kenney, E. J. and Clausen, W. V. (eds) *The Cambridge History of Classical Literature: Vol. 2, Part IV*, Cambridge: Cambridge University Press, pp.420–57.

Knox, P. E. (ed.) (2006) *Oxford Readings in Ovid*, Oxford: Oxford University Press.

Knox, P. E. (ed.) (2009) *A Companion to Ovid*, Malden, MA and Oxford: Blackwell.

Lyne, R. O. A. M. (1980) *The Latin Love Poets from Catullus to Horace*, Oxford: Clarendon Press, pp.239–87.

Sharrock, A. and Ash, R. (2002) *Fifty Key Classical Authors*, London: Routledge, pp.282–91.

Translating Latin Verse

There are several techniques and matters to bear in mind when translating Latin verse, a handful of which are outlined below. The most important thing to remember, however, is that poetic Latin is still Latin and so the familiar and fundamental rules and approaches can be applied in much the same way as when dealing with prose. Accurately translating verse, with its fluid word order and elevated register, is above all the ultimate test of vocabulary, accidence and syntax.

What follows is by no means an exhaustive catalogue and there are plenty of other peculiarities of Latin verse which the student will meet through the passages of this book and beyond.

Vocabulary

As in English, the lexicon of Latin poetry is different to that of prose. There are many words in Ovid which simply do not occur in the widely-read prose authors: for obvious reasons, words for 'radiant' and 'nymph', stories of goddesses and rich descriptions of rural idylls do not feature commonly in Caesar or Cicero.

A list of 450 of the most common items of verse vocabulary can be found at the back of this book. But in addition to learning these words thoroughly, it is highly advisable to make a note of other unfamiliar words encountered in the passages. It need hardly be stressed that not knowing the meaning of words is the greatest obstacle to producing an elegant and accurate translation.

Word order

There are patterns in prose word order to which readers quickly become accustomed (i.e. the verb at the end, nouns with their adjectives, etc.). In verse, however, these rules of thumb no longer pertain. Words will often appear 'out of position' (from a prose point of view) and much more careful analysis will be needed to discover the order of translation. Above all, do not succumb to the temptation to translate each Latin word in the order it appears in the line, a temptation especially powerful when the meaning of a line is difficult to grasp at the first attempt.

The most common challenge is the mix of adjectives and nouns across a sentence. Here is an example:

tantus caelesti venit ab ore vigor.

Such great force came from the heavenly mouth.

Fasti IV.542

In prose, this would be *tantus vigor ab ore caelesti venit* and easily translatable. But in verse, the jumbled word order necessitates care and confidence in accidence to know that *tantus* and *vigor* are both nominative singular (so agree) and that *caelesti* and *ore* are both ablative singular (so agree and follow *ab*).

Often sense will help, but not always in the sometimes obscure and whimsical world of Ovid. Verse requires even better knowledge of accidence than prose to guarantee getting the sense of each sentence.

Key words out of place

As part of the looser word order of verse, a special feature to get used to is the appearance of vital words which introduce new constructions or syntactical units 'out of position'; requiring special care are words

like *qui, quae, quod* (who, which) and conjunctions (*et, ut, cum*, etc.).
Here is an example:

> *ardet <u>ut</u> ad magnos pinea taeda deos.*

Her. XII.34

Accustomed to translating prose, the word order here could easily
lead us along the lines of 'it burned in order to . . .' or 'it burned as . . .'.
In Latin poetry, however, it is very common for a conjunction such as
ut to be postponed from the start of the line, even though that is where
it belongs (again from a prose point of view). So this line translates, 'as
a pine torch burns to the great gods'.

Beware of this: a reader fresh from prose will need to adjust his
expectations regarding where conjunctions will appear.

In a similar vein, be careful when dealing with prepositions, which
in prose generally come before their noun but which in verse can
be moved around much more freely, so that the noun can even
precede the preposition which governs it (a phenomenon known as
anastrophe).

> *. . . nudam pressi corpus ad usque meum.*

I pressed the naked girl right up to my body.
(In prose: . . . *usque ad corpus meum*)

Am. I.5.24

Omission (ellipsis) of verbs

One of the hardest aspects of verse translation is the poet's tendency to
leave out key verbs and ask the reader to 'understand' or 'supply' them.

> *gratia, Musa, tibi.*

Tr. IV.10.117

This verbless sentence requires the translator to add something in: here the best translation is probably 'Thanks <u>be</u> to you, Muse'. As this simple example indicates, an especially common ellipsis is that of the verb 'to be', which can even be left out when it is part of another verb (e.g. a perfect passive).

nescius haec umeris arma parata suis.

Not knowing that these weapons <u>were</u> prepared for his shoulders.

Ars Am. II.50

The infinitive *esse* is omitted (*parata esse* becomes just *parata*). As with so many of verse's peculiarities, practice and care will soon accustom the newcomer to missing verbs.

Omission (ellipsis) of prepositions

As common as omitted verbs are omitted prepositions. Poets frequently miss these little words out altogether and rely on the reader to understand them.

Scylla loco mansit . . .

Scylla stayed in the place . . .

Met. XIV.70

Here, the word *in*, which would be expected in prose, is omitted. The ablative *loco* and common sense point to the correct translation.

Plural for singular

Latin poetry often uses a plural noun when the singular is meant. The only way to tell is by the sense of the sentence – the plural will normally sound very odd in English.

flecte, precor, vult<u>us</u> ad mea furta tu<u>os</u>!

Turn, I pray, your face to my secret missions!
[*lit.* your face<u>s</u>]

Her. XVIII.64

In Ovid, this phenomenon is especially common with the first person, where *nos* (we) and *noster* (our) are regularly used to mean 'I' or 'my' respectively (a sort of 'royal we').

impia si <u>nostros</u> legisset Scylla libellos . . .

If wicked Scylla had read <u>my</u> little books . . .
[*lit.* <u>our</u> little books]

Rem. Am. 67

(Note the conjunction *si* out of place as well.)

It is also worth bearing in mind that, although it is less common, a 'singular for plural' is also found in Ovid (i.e. sometimes the poet uses a singular noun where a plural is strictly meant).

. . . et tacit<u>o</u> pector<u>e</u> multa movent.

. . . and they stir many things in their silent heart<u>s</u>.
[*lit.* silent heart]

Ars Am. I.110

Lines and couplets

When first reading Latin poetry, it can be easy to view each line as a self-contained unit and the end of the line, whether punctuated or not, as a break in syntax. It is not at all necessary, however, for the end of the line to coincide with the end of the clause or sentence and the beginner must quickly disabuse himself of any assumption on this front.

In hexameter poetry, this enjambment is extremely common and the translator will quickly become accustomed to sense flowing from line into line uninterrupted.

plura locuturum timido Peneia cursu
fugit cumque ...

As he was about to say more, Daphne at a frightened run
fled from him and when ...

Met. I.525

In elegiac poetry, the couplet is almost always a complete syntactical
unit. Nevertheless, care is required not to see the end of the first line
(the hexameter) as a necessary break in sense, even if punctuated,
and consideration of the couplet as a whole will often be needed to
translate.

victor abes, nec scire mihi, quae causa morandi,
   aut in quo lateas ferreus orbe, <u>licet</u>.

Though victorious you are still away, nor <u>is it allowed</u> for me to
   know what is the cause of your delay,
or in what part of the world you are hiding, hard-hearted man.

Her. I.57

Looseness of tense

Ovid's abrupt changes of tense from the past to the 'historic' present,
used to add vividness to the Latin, can be disconcerting to translate.
There is certainly no need for a present tense translation in English for
every present tense verb in Latin: keeping everything in the past is
often preferable.

rex populo praedae signa petita <u>dedit</u>.
protinus <u>exsiliunt</u> ...

The king <u>gave</u> the long-awaited sign to the people to grab their
spoils.

They jumped up at once . . .
[*lit.* They jump up . . .].

Ars Am. I.114

Metonymy

Ancient poets use gods or goddesses to represent their attributes or areas of power: this is known as metonymy. It is therefore important to be ready to translate, for example, *Venus* or *Cupido* as 'love', if doing so improves the sense of the English. Similarly *Mars* often means 'war', *Musa* 'poetry', *Ceres* 'corn', and so on.

Tyrrhenum valido Marte per agmen eunt.

They go through the Etruscan column with powerful fighting.

Fasti II.208

Objects can be used to the same effect: so *sceptrum* (sceptre) can stand as metonymy for royal power and *torus* (marriage-bed) or *thalamus* (bed-chamber) for marriage.

In a similar manner, the natural elements are very often personified as divine beings rather than mere physical phenomena: the dawn as *Aurora*, the sun as *Sol* and, most frequently, the various winds such as *Zephyrus*, *Eurus* and *Notus*. These instances of personification need not be undone when translating (*Aurora* can remain as 'Dawn'), but they do require a little care to ensure a smooth and comprehensible translation. Note also that *Amor* is a common alternative name for Cupid.

Finally, be alert for synecdoche, where a part represents the whole. Thus *puppis* (stern) and *prora* (prow) are both used to mean 'ship', *limen* (threshold) to mean a 'house', *axis* (an axle) to mean a 'chariot', and so forth.

Register

As one would expect, there is generally a more elevated and poetical 'register' or tone in Ovid, markedly different to Caesar's accounts of his victories in battle or even the more finely-wrought passages of Cicero or Livy. Poetry's subject matter is naturally less mundane and more inclined to be fantastical, sensual and emotional.

> *mons ibi verticibus petit arduus astra duobus* . . .

> There a high mountain reaches up to the stars with twin peaks . . .
> *Met. I.316*

Sentences of this nature, rich in descriptive detail, hyperbole and personification, are not common in prose but abound in verse. This means there is a need to familiarize oneself with stylistic figures (assonance, asyndeton, polyptoton, etc.) and to translate them idiomatically – as in the example below:

> . . . *deposito pariter cum veste timore* . . .

> . . . having laid aside my fear along with my clothes . . .
> *Her. XVIII.57*

Here we have a fine example of Ovidian wit in the form of zeugma, which requires a confident approach to produce a good translation. In addition, noticing and analysing Ovid's deployment of such stylistic features is vital to appreciating his art and commenting on it (see chapter on *Ovid's Style*).

Deducing the meaning of unfamiliar words

In the passages of this book there will be Latin words which are not familiar, nor listed in the vocabulary checklists, nor glossed. The meanings of such words, however, should be deducible from the context of the passages, or from English or Latin cognates.

An ability to work out some words is simply expected from linguistic general knowledge. So, knowing the meaning of *locus*, the verb *locavit* should not be difficult to translate. What part of the body is the *femur*? Or what is a sword if described as *acutum*? Or can French help in working out the meaning of *fenestra*?

It is also very important when encountering unknown vocabulary to think carefully about how Latin works. A few common facets of the language which can be helpful are given below.

Vowel weakening

First, bear in mind the phenomenon of 'vowel weakening', whereby the vowel sound in a word changes when a prefix is added. This is particularly common with the letter -*a*-, which weakens to -*i*-:

> *facio* becomes *interficio*; *iacio* becomes *adicio*; *salio* becomes *insilio*

But it also happens with other vowels and diphthongs:

> *teneo* becomes *retineo*; *claudo* becomes *includo*

And it occurs in prefixed adjectives as well, especially after the privative *in*-:

> *arma* gives us *inermis*; *aptus* becomes *ineptus*

Be particularly careful when dealing with the stem -*cid*- in a compound verb, as this could be from *caedo* (I kill) or from *cado* (I fall). Therefore the same word can have essentially opposite meanings and consideration of the context will be necessary:

> *caedo* becomes *occido* (I kill); *cado* becomes *occido* (I die)

Scansion, when learnt, can help here: the diphthong in *caedo* gives a long *i* (*occīdo*), whereas the short *a* of *cădo* gives a short *i* (*occĭdo*).

Assimilation

Remember how prefixes work in compound verbs, and look out for assimilation (when the first consonant of a word can induce the final consonant of a prefix to change):

> *ad-cedo* becomes *accedo*; *ex-fodio* becomes *effodio*

Common suffixes

Certain suffixes (endings) can be added to word roots to give a particular effect.

- The suffixes *-tor* (gen. *-toris*), *-sor* (*-soris*) or the feminine *-trix* (*-tricis*) indicate agency, the person who does an action, like the English -er (teacher) or -or (benefactor):

emptor (*emo*)	buyer
victrix (*vinco*)	victor
obsessor (*obsideo*)	besieger

- Fourth declension nouns formed from the supine stem of a verb commonly express the activity the verb denotes:

monitus	warning
ductus	leadership

- The suffixes *-tio* (gen. *-tionis*), *-tudo* (*-tudinis*), *-tia* (*-tiae*), *-tas* (*-tatis*) all form abstract nouns:

libertas (*liber*)	freedom
proditio (*prodo*)	betrayal
claritudo (*clarus*)	fame

- The suffixes *-ellus*, *-ulus*/*-ullus* or *-olus*/*-ollus* indicate diminutives (little or affectionately-viewed versions of the original noun):

filiolus (*filius*)	(dear) little son
libellus (*liber*)	little book

Some final little things

There are a few other aspects to Latin verse language which are worth bearing in mind:

- The ending -*ere* can be used for the third person plural of the perfect active (i.e. instead of -*erunt*):

  amav<u>ere</u> = *amav<u>erunt</u>*   they loved

- The ending -*ere* can also be used instead of -*eris* in the second person singular of the passive (present or future):

  ama<u>bere</u> = *ama<u>beris</u>*   you will be loved

- The genitive plural ending of the second declension can be contracted to -*um* (instead of -*orum*):

  div<u>um</u> = *div<u>orum</u>*   of the gods

- The 'syncopated' form of the perfect or pluperfect tense substitutes -*arat* for -*averat* etc. (i.e. the -*ve*- or -*vi*- is omitted):

  ama<u>rat</u> = *ama<u>verat</u>*   he had loved

  ama<u>sse</u> = *ama<u>visse</u>*   to have loved

- The agreement of the verb with the noun in terms of number can be based on sense rather than strict grammatical accuracy (especially with collective nouns). In the example below, although the subject *turba* is singular, the verbs have plural endings (-*ant*/-*ent*) on the logic that the crowd is made up of many men:

  tura ferant placentque novum pia turba Quirinum

  Let the dutiful crowd bring incense and appease the new Quirinus.

  Fasti II.507

- Two common uses of the accusative case:
  - (i) the 'accusative of respect', where a noun is placed in the accusative to indicate the part (often a body part) affected by the action of the verb:

caput niveo velatus amictu

Having veiled <u>his head</u> with a white hood

(*lit.* Veiled with respect to his head . . .).

Fasti III.363

(ii) the 'exclamatory accusative', where a noun or phrase in the accusative forms an exclamation:

me miserum!   Wretched me!

Ovid's Style

The below does not aspire to be a handbook for the stylistic analysis of Ovid nor to comprise an exhaustive catalogue of his techniques. It is merely intended to point out some elements which the newcomer to Ovid may like to consider both as he reads Ovid's poetry and as he is asked to examine how the poet achieves certain effects.

Several of the books listed on pp.14–15 feature chapters on the style of Ovid. The surest understanding of Ovid's art, however, will come from reading his works as widely and as carefully as possible. Try not to view the passages in this book as chunks of impenetrable Latin to be doggedly translated; rather strive, especially as confidence with the language grows, to notice some of the devices detailed below, and above all to ask how they contribute to the poem's meaning and power in their particular contexts.

Syntax

Anacoluthon

The breaking off of the sentence structure to create the '...' effect of unfinished syntax. This is often used to represent extremes of passion, where the speaker's distraction in the heat of anger, love, etc. leaves his sentence to peter out.

> *invida vestis eras, quae tam bona crura tegebas;*
> *quoque magis spectes – invida vestis eras.*

You were a jealous dress, who covered such fine legs;
  the more one looks ..., oh you were a jealous dress!

Am. III.2.27

In his lustful reveries about the legs beneath his girl's dress, the anacoluthon suggests the speaker has lost his train of thought entirely.

Anaphora

The repetition of the same word (or phrase), generally at the start of successive clauses. The effect is a rhetorical one, often adding insistence or emphasis by the hammering repetition of a particular detail.

te maestae volucres, Orpheu, te turba ferarum,
te rigidi silices, te carmina saepe secutae
fleverunt silvae . . .

For you, Orpheus, wept the sad birds, for you the throng of beasts,
for you the hard flints, for you the woods who had often followed
your songs . . .

Met. XI.44

The repeated *te* before each new subject underlines the single focus of all of nature's grief on 'you' (i.e. Orpheus). Anaphora is often (as here) combined with asyndeton (on which see below).

Apostrophe

The 'turning away' of the narrator or speaker from his narrative to address a character, an object or the reader.

at te, Nesse ferox, eiusdem virginis ardor
perdiderat volucri traiectum terga sagitta.

But you, fierce Nessus, had passion for the same
maiden destroyed, pierced through the back by a winged arrow.

Met. IX.101

In this example, the fate of Nessus is made more dramatic and immediate by the narrator's direct address of the centaur just before he describes how he met his end. But apostrophe can have other effects: it can arouse pity, as is the case above with the apostrophe of Orpheus from *Met. XI*, while in the example from *Am. III* its impact is comic as Ovid lecherously apostrophizes a dress.

Asyndeton

The omission of conjunctions. Again, the effects of asyndeton are manifold, but often it can add rhetorical power to a list (it is often combined with anaphora – see the example from *Met. XI* above) or generate speed in a string of clauses.

> *tum bis ad occasus, bis se convertit ad ortus,*
> *ter iuvenem baculo tetigit, tria carmina dixit.*

> The she turned herself twice to the west, twice to the east,
> thrice she touched the youth with her wand, she spoke three spells.
>
> *Met. XIV.386*

Here the asyndeton helps to recreate the witch Circe's formulaic incantations, following one after the other in ritual succession.

Hendiadys

The expression of one complex idea as though two separate ones. This commonly serves to magnify or to emphasize.

> *quid tibi de <u>turba</u> narrem <u>numeroque</u> virorum?*

> What can I tell you about the huge crowd of men?
> [*lit.* the crowd and the number of men]
>
> *Her. XVI.183*

The separation of the idea of a 'big crowd' into two elements, 'crowd' and 'number', exaggerates the size of the throng.

Hypallage

The use of an adjective to describe a noun with which it does not properly belong (also known as 'transferred epithet').

> *ecce boves illuc Erytheidas adplicat heros*
> *emensus <u>longi</u> claviger <u>orbis iter</u>.*

Look! The club-bearing hero drives the Erythean
oxen here, travelling a <u>long journey through the world</u>.
[*lit.* a journey through the long world]

Fasti I.543

By the transferring of the adjective *longi* from *iter* to *orbis*, the Latin seems to emphasize the world-spanning length of Hercules' trek.

Litotes

Double negation, producing understatement for effect.

> *qua venata foret silva, narrare parantem*
> *impedit amplexu <u>nec</u> se <u>sine crimine</u> prodit.*

As she prepared to tell which woods she hunted in,
he stopped her by his embrace and betrayed himself <u>in all his villainy</u>.
[*lit.* not without a crime]

Met. II.432

Jupiter's abject criminality as he rapes Callisto is stressed by the deliberately inadequate double negative *nec . . . sine crimine.*

Paronomasia

A pun or play on words with similar sounds.

> *illa sonat raucum quiddam atque inamabile <u>ridet</u>,*
>   *ut <u>rudit</u> a scabra turpis asella mola.*

> That girl makes a harsh sound and she <u>laughs</u> horribly,
>   as a mangy ass <u>brays</u> by a rough mill-stone.

> *Ars Am. III.289*

The play on the similar-sounding verbs *ridet* (laughs) and *rudit* (brays) makes humorously indistinguishable the laughter of the girl and the bestial grunting of a donkey.

Polyptoton

The repetition of different inflections of the same word.

> *flagrabant sancti sceleratis <u>ignibus ignes</u>,*
>   *mixtaque erat <u>flammae flamma</u> profana piae.*

> The sacred <u>fires</u> were burning with accursed <u>fires</u>,
>   and unholy <u>flame</u> had been mixed with pious <u>flame</u>.

> *Fasti VI.439*

The strangeness of the scene as the fires of Rome's sacred hearth in the temple of Vesta are 'burnt' in a fire (i.e. the temple itself is burning down), as well as the profusion of flames in this roaring inferno, is conveyed by the double polyptoton.

Polysyndeton

The exaggerated use of conjunctions (contrast to <u>a</u>syndeton). Its effect is primarily to magnify a list, often of places or people but also of actions or events.

> *iam Samos a laeva (fuerant Naxosque relictae*
>   *et Paros et Clario Delos amata deo)*
> *dextra Lebinthos erat silvisque umbrosa Calymne*
>   *cinctaque piscosis Astypalaea vadis . . .*

> Now Samos was on their left (Naxos and Paros and Delos
>   loved by the Clarian god had been left behind)
> Lebinthos was on their right and Calymne shaded with woods
>   and Astypalaea surrounded with fish-filled shallows . . .

Ars Am. II.79

The repeated *et* and *-que* exaggerate the catalogue of islands dotting the sea far below Daedalus and Icarus as they soar along above them.

Proper nouns and antonomasia

Throughout the *Metamorphoses* especially, the reader will note the number of times that a character's name is not used. Instead, Ovid conjures an epic atmosphere with antonomasia (using a different appellation), including geographical epithets (e.g. *Delius* for Apollo), patronymics (e.g. *Pelides* for Achilles – look out for the *-ides* suffix) and simply roles or titles (e.g. *rector maris* for Neptune). Often, however, more is at play than mere 'epicizing', and particular names are used at significant moments.

> *neque enim Iove nata recusat*
> *nec monet ulterius nec iam certamina differt.*

> Nor did the daughter of Jupiter refuse,
> nor make further warnings nor delay the contest.

Met. VI.51

Ovid's description of Athene by the epic antonomasia *Iove nata* at this moment underlines Arachne's audacity as she fearlessly challenges so great a goddess to a weaving contest. And as ever in Ovid, there is often a sense of parody in his use of such epic devices.

et notos mores non satis urbis habet
in qua Martigenae non sunt sine crimine nati
Romulus <u>Iliades Iliades</u>que Remus.

And he does not know well enough this city's customs,
in which the sons of Mars were born with no little scandal,
Romulus the <u>son of Ilia</u> and <u>the son of Ilia</u> Remus.

Am. III.4.38

Here Ovid's rather outrageous contention is that adultery is authentically Roman, sanctioned and sanctified by the ancient myths of the city's foundation. The very epic compound adjective *Martigenae* and the repeated patronymic *Iliades* give a humorous grandeur as Ovid teases his serious forebears who had epicized Rome's glorious rise (and, more daringly, his contemporaries who were trying to re-energize these myths). Note the litotes here too, of course, in *non . . . sine crimine nati*.

Finally, remember how proper nouns can be used in metonymy or personification to add a poetic grandeur, sincere or tongue-in-cheek, to simple objects or abstractions (see earlier section for details).

Tricolon

A succession of three parallel words or clauses. The last is often the longest or most powerful: this is known as a tricolon crescens or crescendo. It is often combined with asyndeton and/or anaphora, as in the example below:

non incola montis,
non ego sum pastor, non hic armenta gregesque
horridus observo.

I am not a mountain dweller,
nor a shepherd, nor am I some unkempt fellow watching over
the herds and flocks here.

Met. I.512

The tricolon crescens in this example adds rhetorical power as the god Apollo makes very clear to Daphne that he is far from being some common-or-garden local peasant.

Zeugma (or syllepsis)

Usually in Ovid, the use of one verb with two subjects or objects of differing natures (generally one literal, the other metaphorical). Its effect is a witty linking of the two, often to convey the combined physical and mental impact of a single event.

> *et mens et quod opus fabrilis dextra tenebat*
> *excidit:*

> Both his sense and the work his craftsman's hand was holding
> fell away ...

Met. IV.175

So here, as he sees Venus and Mars *in flagrante delicto*, Vulcan's mental faculties metaphorically 'drop away' and at the same time the iron he is forging literally drops from his hand: in other words, the zeugma pithily describes how he reeled utterly, body and soul, at what he saw.

Word order

Chiasmus

The ordering of words or phrases in an 'A-B-B-A' arrangement. Chiasmus' effects are legion, though it often enacts a sense of contrast or balance.

A   B   B   A

ventus erat nautis aptus, non aptus amanti.

The wind was well-suited to sailors, not well-suited to a lover.

Her. XIII.11

The chiastic arrangement above emphasizes the antithesis: the wind is perfect for the sailors in their eagerness to set sail, but hateful to Laodamia, as it will bear her husband's ship from her. Although this particular use of chiasmus, to stress a contrast, is a common one, chiastic arrangement can achieve other effects too:

A   B   C   C   B   A
candida me capiet, capiet me flava puella.

A pale-skinned girl will captivate me, a blond will captivate me.
Am. II.4.39

In this instance the chiasmus, combined with the repeated *capiet* and *me*, underlines how catholic is Ovid's taste in girls.

Epanalepsis

The resumptive repetition of a word or phrase after intervening words, often on the next line of verse.

nec tibi, quae reditus monstrarent, fila dedissem,
  fila per adductas saepe recepta manus.

I wish I had not given you the <u>thread</u> to show you the route back,
  <u>thread</u> often taken up again and passed through the hands it led.
Her. X.103

The epanalepsis helps to generate a plangent tone in Ariadne's words as she proclaims her regret at having given the thread, the very thread (stressed by its repetition) which had saved Theseus' life in the Labyrinth. Although, as several scholars note, epanalepsis is comparatively rare in Ovid, it does feature in several of the passages of this book and in his works more widely, generally with the effect of adding emphasis or emotional weight to the repeated word or phrase.

Hyperbaton

The disruption of normal word order to engineer a separation of words which syntactically belong together.

> *et pavidum blandita 'fer has, fidissime, <u>nostro</u>—'*
> *dixit, et adiecit longo post tempore '<u>fratri</u>.'*

And said in fearfully coaxing tones, 'Take this, most trusty servant, to my ...', and she added after a long pause '... brother'.

> *Met. IX.569*

In this famous and remarkable example of hyperbaton, Byblis' embarrassment and fear in revealing that the recipient of her ardent love-letter is to be her own brother is beautifully conveyed by the hyperbaton of *nostro ... fratri* (my ... brother). It is especially effective, as Anderson notes, because *nostro* on its own could mean 'my darling': we have to wait an excruciating line for Byblis to spell out the real addressee of her letter with *fratri*.[1] This delay of a dramatic detail is one of the many effects Ovid achieves by hyperbaton. Another is the suggestion of length or labour as the separation of words draws out the phrase; or simply heavy emphasis, as in this example which sees Iphis berating herself for her unnatural but inescapable love:

> *<u>meus</u> est furiosior illo,*
> *si verum profitemur, <u>amor</u>.*

> <u>My love</u> is more crazed than hers,
> if truth be told.

> *Met. IX.737*

---

[1]   Anderson, W. S. (1972) *Ovid's Metamorphoses: Books 6–10*, Norman, OK: University of Oklahoma Press, pp.457–8.

Iconic word order

The arrangement of words in such an order that they mimic or depict their meaning, so that syntax imitates sense. This is also known as 'pictorial' or 'mimetic' word order.

saepe, ubi constiterant hinc Thisbe,|Pyramus illinc . . .

Often, when on this side had stood Thisbe, Pyramus on that . . .

Met. IV.71

The chiastic word order here is iconic, in that the words draw out the picture of Pyramus and Thisbe either side of the thin party-wall, pressed against it and listening to each other's amorous whispers. A very common species of iconic word order is the enclosing of one phrase within another to enact a sense of surrounding, as in the example below, where the mountain summits are beset on all sides by the surging waters of Jupiter's flood:

pulsabantque novi montana cacumina fluctus.

And the new waves were pounding mountain tops.

Met. I.310

Juxtaposition

The collocation of words for effect (usually contrast).

gratia sic <u>minimo magna</u> labore venit.

Thus great favour comes from very little effort.

Am. III.4.46

The juxtaposed opposites *minimo* and *magna* emphasize the antithesis Ovid is drawing here between the minimal work a liberal-minded husband needs to put in and the immense rewards he can expect to win. This juxtaposition of clashing or antipodal words is a common device to stress contrast, conflict or sudden change.

Metre and rhythm

To reduce Ovid's use of metre to simplistic axioms such as 'dactyls = speed' represents, of course, an utterly inadequate account of the metrical nuances of a genius. Nevertheless, here are some things to consider in analysing the rhythm of lines of Ovid – a vital and often-overlooked area to examine when considering the stylistic effectiveness of a passage. (See *An Introduction to Scansion and Ovid's Metres* for how to scan.)

Dactyls

Dactylic rhythms add pace and momentum to the verse, conveying speed with their 'tripping' or 'galloping' pulse. Here, Actaeon's hounds begin a tearing chase of their one-time master:

$$- \cup \ \cup- \ \cup\cup-\cup \ \cup - - -\cup\cup \ - \ \times$$
inde ruunt alii rapida velocius aura

Then charged the rest, swifter than a howling wind ...

Met. III.209

They can evoke excitement or panic, like a racing heartbeat, as below of Phaethon's terror as his chariot hurtles towards the ground:

$$- \ \cup\cup- \ \cup \ \cup- \ \cup \ \cup \ \ - \ \cup \ \cup-\cup\cup \ -\times$$
palluit et subito genu(a) intremuere timore.

He turned pale and his knees trembled with a sudden fear.

Met. II.180

and similarly distress and emotional turmoil, such as Attis' here:

$$- \ \cup\cup - \cup\cup - , \ \cup \ \cup - \ \ \cup\cup - \cup\cup \ - \ \times$$
et modo 'tolle faces', 'remove' modo 'verbera' clamat.

And she shouted at one moment, 'Take away the torches!', at
another 'Remove the whips!'

Fasti IV.235

Finally, dactyls can give a feeling of lightness to the verse as well as
speed – indeed it is worth noting that, in general, Ovid's hexameters
are significantly more dactylic than (for example) Virgil's. Below,
perhaps, there is a lightness as Ovid recalls his embarrassing impotence
– and perhaps too there is a suggestion of sexual excitement in the
dactyls which is humorously incongruous with the stubborn failure of
his apparatus to perform:

$$- \ \cup \ \cup - \ \ \cup\cup - \cup\cup - \ \ \cup\cup \ - \ \ \ \cup \ \cup - \times$$
tacta tamen veluti gelida mea membra cicuta

$$- \ \cup\cup \ - \ \cup\cup - \ \ \ - \ \cup\cup - \cup \ \ \cup\times$$
segnia propositum destituere meum;

But my member, as though touched by cold hemlock,
  sluggishly resisted my efforts.

Am. III.7.13

Enjambment

The run-on of sense from one line of poetry into another, so the sense
of the one line is completed by a word or phrase at the start of the
next. Enjambment is generally rarer in Ovid's hexameters than in
Virgil's and line-breaks in the former more frequently coincide with
breaks in syntax, but this point should not be overstated, and plenty of
examples of enjambment will present themselves to the reader of
Ovid. The enjambed word is given great weight:

qui, quoniam prohibent anni bellare, loquendo
pugnat et incessit scelerataque devovet arma.

Since his age prevented him from doing battle, by his words
he fought, and advanced and cursed their guilty weapons.

Met. V.101

So here Emathion's determination to fight despite his age is
underlined by the enjambment of *pugnat*. This run-on of the verb can,
with verbs such as 'fall', 'leap down', 'strike', etc., enact the sense as the
verb itself 'drops' into the next line:

tum vero praeceps curru fremebundus ab alto
desilit et . . .

Then indeed with a roar from his high chariot headlong
he leapt down, and . . .

Met. XII.128

Note that the enjambed verb, especially in moments of dramatic
action such as this, is often a dactyl – a particular favourite of Virgil as
well. But it is not always verbs which are emphasized in this way. In
the example below, the power of Alcyone's hysterical, grief-stricken
cries, which prevent her even speaking, is conveyed by the enjambment
and delay of the noun *plangor*, the subject:

plura dolor prohibet, verboque intervenit omni
plangor, et attonito gemitus a corde trahuntur.

Grief stopped her saying more, and interrupting every word was
wailing, and groans rose up from her stricken heart.

Met. XI.708

Enjambment in elegiac couplets, where each line generally and
each couplet almost invariably forms a self-contained syntactical unit,
is much rarer. Nevertheless, allowing a word to run over the end of the
line can lend it significant emphasis, as in the example below where

Ovid dwells on the great good fortune of a lover who can stir jealousy in his girl:

> *o quater et quotiens numero comprendere non est*
> *<u>felicem</u>, de quo laesa puella dolet.*

Four times, so many times that cannot be counted, is he <u>lucky</u>, over whom a wounded girl grieves!

Ars Am. II.447

Spondees

In contrast to the light, swift rhythm of dactyls, spondees are slower, weightier and more solemn: the name itself derives from the Greek σπονδαί (*spondai*), offerings to the gods. In the example below, Ovid reflects the ritual gravitas of the flute-players' roles in Rome in days gone by with the stately spondees:

> — — — — — — — — —∪∪ — ✗
> *cantabat fanis, cantabat tibia ludis,*
>
> — — — — — — —∪∪ — ∪ ∪ ✗
> *cantabat maestis tibia funeribus.*

The flute played at shrines, the flute played at the games,
the flute played at sorrowful funerals.

Fasti VI.659

Naturally, slow spondaic rhythms are commonly employed to evoke slumber:

> — ∪ ∪ — — — — — — —∪ ∪— ✗
> *nox erat, et somnus lassos submisit ocellos.*

It was night, and sleep weighed down my weary eyes.

Am. III.5.1

And of course, in contrast to the effortless pace of dactyls, spondees convey slowness and struggle, as this example shows: first the quick dactyl for the goose's nimble flutter out of the reach of Baucis and

Philemon; and then the plodding, spondaic rhythm which dominates the line as the poor old couple strive in vain to catch up with their intended dinner:

‾⏑ ⏑ ‾ ‾ ‾‾ ‾ ‾ ‾⏑ ⏑‾ ×
ille celer penna tardos aetate fatigat.

The goose, swift with its feathers, wears out the couple made slow by their age.

Met. VIII.686

The slowness of spondees can introduce other ideas too. As Ovid replies to the charge that he should be concerning himself with more serious matters than love elegy, he uses lumbering spondees to convey his boredom at the very thought of the traditional careers:

‾ ‾ ‾ ‾‾ ‾ ‾‾ ‾‾⏑ ⏑ ‾ ×
nec me verbosas leges ediscere nec me

‾ ‾‾ ‾ ‾ ‾ ⏑⏑‾ ⏑ ⏑ ×
ingrato vocem prostituisse foro?

... that I do not learn by heart wordy laws, nor prostitute my voice in the unwelcome forum?

Am. I.15.5

Sound effects

Ovid makes rich and varied use of sound effects in his poetry – never forget that his poems would have been recited as well as read, and so the sound of his words is a vital consideration in analysis of his artistry. Sometimes the sound is onomatopoeic (it mimics the sound being described), as in this famous description of frogs in a pond:

quamvis sint sub aqua, sub aqua maledicere temptant.

Although they are underwater, underwater they try to shout abuse.

Met. VI.376

The consonance of -*qu*- here, in each instance occurring in the stressed syllable at the start of a metrical foot, echoes the guttural croak of the newly-transformed frogs. Or:

candidior nivibus, tunc cum cecidere recentes . . .

Whiter than snow, then when it has recently fallen . . .

Am. III.5.11

with the alliteration of -*c*- evoking the crunch of crisp, new-fallen snow. But such effects are not always mimetic:

. . . et postes extrema cuspide pulsat.
concussae patuere fores.| videt intus edentem
vipereas carnes, vitiorum alimenta suorum,
Invidiam visaque oculos avertit.

. . . and she beat the doors with the head of her spear.
As they were struck the doors opened. Inside she saw Envy,
eating the flesh of serpents, nourishment for her evils,
and she turned away her eyes as she beheld this sight.

Met. II.767

In the first two lines of this passage, the consonance of *c*, *s* and *p* does indeed make the words resound with the crash of Athene's spear, sending the doors of Envy's house flying open. But the *v*-/*vi*-alliteration in the second half could not be said to be recreating a particular sound. Rather, it seems perhaps to evoke a more intangibly ugly and eerie atmosphere. It also ties the various qualities described to *Invidia* (especially her foul meal of snake meat – *vipereas* – and her wickedness – *vitiorum*): this use of alliteration to link words is a common Ovidian technique to look out for. This passage might therefore give a broader picture of some of the ways in which Ovid uses the sound of his words beyond mere mimesis.

It is worth also considering the particular effects of certain sounds. The example above shows the power of plosive consonants (especially *p* and *b*) for striking, pounding or the beat of horses' hooves. The repeated *s*-sound (sibilance) seems to have been inherently unpleasant to ancient ears, and so, as well as echoing snakes' hissing and running water, it can evoke misery, discomfort or ugliness. In the example below, Ovid remembers with evident pain his last night in Rome before departing into exile:

cum subit illius tristissima noctis imago . . .

When the most sorrowful picture of that night comes to my mind . . .

Tr. I.3.1

Conversely, a pleasant, sensual or languid effect can often be achieved by liquids (*l* and *r*). In the example below, Mercury sends Argus to sleep:

languida permulcens medicata lumina virga.

Stroking his drowsy eyes with his sleep-inducing wand.

Met. I.716

The soporific *l*-consonance here, combined with the gentle murmur of *m*, can lull even Argus' one hundred watchful eyes to sleep.

Final note

The examples used above have been deliberately selected from all over Ovid's works to demonstrate as clearly as possible the devices the poet uses. This has inevitably meant that these selections are out of context and that other elements of the Latin have been left unmentioned to focus squarely on the single stylistic feature in question in each example.

A flavour of the context has been given for each quotation here because it is all-important: without understanding what is happening, what Ovid or his characters are saying, noting stylistic effects is a futile exercise. Any appreciation of the style of a passage must be a synthesis of device and effect – not just what is interesting about the Latin but what this achieves and why.

So as confidence begins to grow, the reader must try not only to spot such effects as those outlined above but also to consider what they contribute to Ovid's meaning, being as specific as possible to the context.

Ovid's Elegiac Poetry

Passages 1–20
Shorter translation passages

Passages 21–40
Full translation and comprehension passages

Elegiac Passage 1 *The fame of Arion*

Arion, a famous lyre-player and singer, has made a tour of Italy, in the course of which he has charmed men and beasts alike, as well as winning a fortune for himself. Now he prepares to return home to the island of Lesbos.

The story begins:

quod mare non novit, quae nescit Ariona tellus?
  carmine currentes ille tenebat aquas.
saepe sequens agnam lupus est a voce retentus,
  saepe avidum fugiens restitit agna lupum;
saepe canes leporesque umbra iacuere sub una,   5
  et stetit in saxo proxima cerva leae.
nomen Arionium Siculas impleverat urbes
  captaque erat lyricis Ausonis ora sonis;
inde domum repetens puppem conscendit Arion,
  atque ita quaesitas arte ferebat opes.   10
forsitan, infelix, ventos undasque timebas:
  at tibi nave tua tutius aequor erat.

FASTI II

Arion, -onis (Gk acc. *-ona*) (m.)	Arion
avidus, -a, -um	greedy, hungry
lepus, -oris (m.)	hare
cerva, -ae (f.)	deer, hind
lea, -ae (f.)	lioness
Arionius, -a, -um	of Arion
Siculus, -a, -um	Sicilian, of Sicily
impleo, -ere, -plevi, -pletum	I fill
lyricus, -a, -um	of a lyre (*an ancient harp*)
Ausonis, -idis	Italian
conscendo, -ere, -ndi, -nsum	I board
forsitan	perhaps

DISCENDUM *-ere for -erunt*

In verse, *-ere* is often added to the perfect stem as an alternative ending for the third person plural of the perfect active (i.e. = *-erunt*). So here *iacuere* = *iacuerunt*. Take care not to confuse this with the infinitive (*iacere*).

Note also that the *-eris* ending of the second person singular passive (present or future) can also become *-ere*: so *amabere* = *amaberis* (you will be loved).

Elegiac Passage 2 *Medea worries about Jason*

Medea tells her lover, Jason, how she spent an anxious night worrying about his safety after her father, King Aeëtes, had set him three terrible tasks to win the Golden Fleece.

My father, King Aeëtes, laid out the tasks you had to complete before you received the Golden Fleece: 'to yoke the bulls of Mars; to sow the field with the dragon's teeth; and to conquer the unsleeping serpent.'

dixerat <u>Aeetes</u>: maesti <u>consurgitis</u> omnes,
    mensaque purpureos deserit alta toros.
tristis abis. oculis <u>abeuntem</u> prosequor <u>udis</u>
    et dixit tenui <u>murmure</u> lingua: 'vale!'
ut positum tetigi thalamo male saucia lectum,   5
    <u>acta est</u> per lacrimas nox mihi quanta fuit.
ante oculos taurique meos segetesque nefandae,
    ante meos oculos <u>pervigil</u> <u>anguis</u> erat.
hinc amor, hinc timor est—ipsum timor auget amorem.
    mane erat et thalamo cara recepta soror   10
disiectamque comas aversaque in ora iacentem
    invenit et lacrimis omnia plena meis.

                  HEROIDES XII

Aeetes, -is (m.)	King Aeëtes
consurgo, -ere, -surrexi, -surrectum	I stand up (together)
abeuntem	*supply* 'te'
udus, -a, -um	moist, wet
murmur, -uris (n.)	murmur
ago, -ere, egi, actum	*(of time)* I spend
pervigil, -ilis	ever-watchful
anguis, -is (c.)	snake

DISCENDUM *Adjectival agreement*

One of the greatest challenges of verse is piecing together adjectives and nouns in a line to find what agrees with what. Line 2 here is a good example; despite the difficult word order, you need to spot that *mensa* agrees with *alta* (feminine singular nominative), and *purpureos* with *toros* (masculine plural accusative). You must be very focused on endings in verse and cannot rely on adjectives being next to their nouns, as they often are in prose.

Elegiac Passage 3 *Rape of the Sabine Women I*

The early Romans under King Romulus have no women. They therefore invite a neighbouring tribe, the Sabines, to attend games in Rome, with the intention of stealing the Sabine womenfolk and taking them as their own wives.

The Roman people sat on seating made of turf, their unkempt hair crowned with whatever leaves they could find.

respiciunt, oculisque <u>notant</u> sibi quisque puellam
    quam velit, et tacito pectore multa movent.
in medio <u>plausu</u> (<u>plausus</u> tunc arte carebant)
    rex populo praedae signa petita dedit.
protinus exsiliunt, animum clamore <u>fatentes</u>,   5
    virginibus <u>cupidas</u> iniciuntque manus.
ut fugiunt aquilas, timidissima turba, columbae,
    ut fugit invisos agna <u>novella</u> lupos,
sic illae timuere viros <u>sine more</u> ruentes;
    <u>constitit</u> in nulla qui fuit ante color.   10
nam timor unus erat, <u>facies</u> non una timoris:
    pars laniat crines, pars sine mente sedet;
altera maesta <u>silet</u>, frustra vocat altera matrem:
    haec queritur, stupet haec; haec manet, illa fugit.

                    ARS AMATORIA I

noto, -are, -avi, -atum	I make a note of, mark
plausus, -us (m.)	applause
fateor, -eri, fassus sum	I confess, reveal
cupidus, -a, -um	eager, lustful
novellus, -a, -um	young
sine more	unrestrainedly
consisto, -ere, -stiti, -stitum	(*here*) I remain
facies, -ei (f.)	appearance, manifestation
sileo, -ere, -ui	I am silent

DISCENDUM *Omission of prepositions*

Prepositions, like verbs, are omitted much more often in verse than in prose. You need to use your common sense to arrive at a good translation when a preposition is missing. In line 2, *tacito pectore* is best translated as 'in their silent hearts': you need to spot the ablative and think carefully to work out that *in* + abl. is missing.

Note also here that *tacito pectore* is an example of poetic singular for plural.

Elegiac Passage 4 *Rape of the Sabine Women II*

War soon breaks out with the Sabine men, incensed at the rape of their daughters. But in this passage, the Sabine women reconcile their fathers and their new husbands.

King Romulus' Sabine wife encouraged the other women to take action in the forthcoming battle, and so they prepared themselves.

iam steterant acies ferro mortique paratae,
   iam <u>lituus</u> pugnae signa daturus erat,
cum <u>raptae</u> veniunt inter patresque virosque,
   inque sinu natos, <u>pignora</u> cara, tenent.
ut medium campi <u>scissis</u> tetigere capillis,   5
   in terram posito <u>procubuere</u> genu;
et, quasi sentirent, <u>blando</u> clamore <u>nepotes</u>
   tendebant ad <u>avos</u> bracchia parva suos.
qui poterat, clamabat 'avum' tum denique visum,
   et, qui vix poterat, posse coactus erat.   10
tela viris animique cadunt, gladiisque <u>remotis</u>
   dant <u>soceri</u> <u>generis</u> accipiuntque manus,
laudatasque tenent natas, scutoque <u>nepotem</u>
   fert <u>avus</u>: hic scuti dulcior usus erat.

                         FASTI III

lituus, -i (m.)	trumpet
raptae, -arum (f.pl.)	the stolen women
pignus, -oris (n.)	pledge of love; child
scindo, -ere, scidi, scissum	I tear
procumbo, -ere, -cubui, -cubitum	I bend down
blandus, -a, -um	charming, endearing
nepos, -otis (m.)	grandson
avus, -i (m.)	grandfather
removeo, -ere, -movi, -motum	I lay aside
socer, -eri (m.)	father-in-law
gener, -eri (m.)	son-in-law

DISCENDUM *Zeugma*

In your study of Latin literature, you will have encountered figures of speech such as zeugma. Now you will be meeting devices like this unseen in Ovid's poetry. You must aim to be able to pick them out and comment on their stylistic effect; but you must also be able to find a good English translation for them. Have a think about how best to translate the zeugma of *tela viris animique cadunt* in line 11 of this passage.

Elegiac Passage 5 *The soldiery of love*

Ovid tells his students of love that their lives will be like those of soldiers: they need to be prepared to endure many hardships and use all their initiative to get their girl.

Be hardy: do not be put off by the scorching heat of
summer nor by a road white with fallen snow.

militiae species amor est; discedite, <u>segnes</u>:
    non sunt haec timidis signa <u>tuenda</u> viris.
nox et hiems longaeque viae saevique dolores
    mollibus his castris et labor omnis inest.
saepe feres <u>imbrem</u> caelesti nube <u>solutum</u>,   5
    frigidus et nuda saepe iacebis humo.
si tibi per tutum planumque negabitur ire,
    atque erit opposita ianua <u>fulta</u> <u>sera</u>,
at tu <u>per praeceps</u> tecto <u>delabere</u> aperto:
    det quoque <u>furtivas</u> alta <u>fenestra</u> vias.   10
laeta erit, et causam tibi se sciet esse pericli;
    hoc dominae certi <u>pignus</u> amoris erit.
saepe tua poteras, <u>Leandre</u>, carere puella:
    transnabas, animum nosset ut illa tuum.

                  ARS AMATORIA II

segnis, -e	slow, lazy
tueor, -eri, tutus sum	I guard
imber, imbris (m.)	rain
solvo, -ere, -vi, -utum	(*here*) I let loose, fall
fulcio, -ire, fulsi, fultum	I fasten
sera, -ae (f.)	bolt
per praeceps	headlong
delabor, -i, -lapsus sum	I slip down (*-ere = -eris*)
furtivus, -a, -um	secret
fenestra, -ae (f.)	window
pignus, -oris (n.)	token, pledge
Leander, -ri (m.)	Leander (*who swam across the Hellespont to see his lover, Hero*)

DISCENDUM *The syncopated perfect and pluperfect*

It is very common in verse to see the so-called 'syncopated' form of the pluperfect tense, where a syllable is missed out. In line 14, notice how the pluperfect subjunctive *novisset* becomes just *nosset* (i.e. the *-vi-* vanishes). This also happens in the indicative (*amaverat* becomes just *amarat*) and the perfect infinitive (*amavisse* becomes *amasse*). Watch out: it can be a little disconcerting.

Elegiac Passage 6 *Daedalus plans his escape*

The master craftsman Daedalus, being held captive on Crete by King Minos, prepares for a daring escape by air, while his young son Icarus looks on.

Daedalus pleaded with Minos to allow him and his son Icarus to return home, but Minos had no intention of allowing them to go.

quod simul ac sensit, 'nunc, nunc, o <u>Daedale</u>,' dixit:
    '<u>materiam</u>, qua sis <u>ingeniosus</u>, habes.
possidet et terras et possidet aequora <u>Minos</u>:
    nec tellus nostrae nec patet unda fugae.
<u>restat</u> iter caeli: caelo temptabimus ire.   5
    da <u>veniam</u> <u>coepto</u>, Iuppiter alte, meo:
non ego sidereas <u>adfecto</u> tangere sedes:
    qua fugiam dominum, nulla, nisi ista, via est.'
ingenium <u>mala</u> saepe movent: quis crederet umquam
    <u>aerias</u> hominem carpere posse vias?   10
<u>tractabat</u> <u>ceram</u>que puer pennasque <u>renidens</u>,
    nescius haec umeris arma parata suis.
cui pater 'his' inquit 'patria est adeunda carinis,
    hac nobis <u>Minos</u> effugiendus ope.'

ARS AMATORIA II

Daedalus, -i (m.)	Daedalus
materia, -ae (f.)	(*here*) opportunity
ingeniosus, -a, -um	clever, ingenious
Minos, -oi (m.)	Minos (*king of Crete*)
resto, -are, -stiti	I remain
venia, -ae (f.)	pardon
coeptum, -i (n.)	undertaking, plan
adfecto, -are, -avi, -atum	I aspire
mala, -orum (n.pl.)	adversity, troubles
aerius, -a, -um	of the air
tracto, -are, -avi, -atum	I handle
cera, -ae (f.)	wax
renideo, -ere	I smile

DISCENDUM *Ellipsis of verbs*

The omission (ellipsis) of verbs, especially the verb 'to be', is a regular feature of Latin verse. So in line 12, the infinitive *esse* has been missed out; you need to understand it when translating (*parata <u>esse</u>*).

Elegiac Passage 7 *Hypermnestra tries to kill Lynceus*

Hypermnestra and her 49 sisters married their cousins, but were ordered by their father to murder them once they were wed. They all obeyed except Hypermnestra; here, she tells her husband Lynceus why she could not kill him.

You were lying there asleep, for the wine I had
given to you was the wine of slumber.

excussere metum violenti iussa parentis;
  erigor et capio tela tremente manu.
non ego falsa loquar. ter acutum sustulit ensem,
  ter male sublato reccidit ense manus.
admovi iugulo (sine me tibi vera fateri!)   5
  admovi iugulo tela paterna tuo;
sed timor et pietas crudelibus obstitit ausis
  castaque mandatum dextra refugit opus.
purpureos laniata sinus, laniata capillos
  exiguo dixi talia verba sono: 10
'saevus, Hypermnestra, pater est tibi; iussa parentis
  effice; germanis sit comes iste suis!
quin age dumque iacet, fortes imitare sorores;
  credibile est caesos omnibus esse viros.'

HEROIDES XIV

violentus, -a, -um	cruel
erigo, -ere, erexi, erectum	I raise up
acutus, -a, -um	sharp
iugulum, -i (n.)	throat
obsto, -are, -stiti, -statum (+ dat.)	I get in the way of, prevent
ausum, -i (n.)	daring deed
castus, -a, -um	chaste, virtuous
lanio, -are, -avi, -atum	I tear at
germanus, -i (m.)	brother
quin age	but come now
imitor, -ari, -atus sum	I imitate

DISCENDUM *Looseness of tense*

In verse you will often see abrupt changes of tense from the past to the 'historic' present. This is used to add vividness to the Latin, but it can be disconcerting to translate. So here we lurch from the perfect *excussere* (remember -*ere* = -*erunt*) to the presents *erigor* and *capio*. Don't be confused – just find the best English translation (normally keeping everything in the past).

Elegiac Passage 8 *Leander and Hero*

Leander, kept from swimming to his lover Hero by the weather, remembers the first time he swam to her, and how he invoked the aid of Luna, the Moon-goddess, appealing to her memory of how she loved the shepherd Endymion.

The sea is too rough – how I wish I could fly like Daedalus!

interea, dum cuncta negant ventique fretumque,
   mente agito furti tempora prima mei.
nox erat incipiens—namque est meminisse voluptas—
   cum foribus patriis egrediebar amans.
nec mora, deposito pariter cum veste timore,   5
   iactabam liquido bracchia lenta mari.
luna fere tremulum praebebat lumen eunti
   ut comes in nostras officiosa vias.
hanc ego suspiciens, 'faveas, dea candida,' dixi,
   'et subeant animo Latmia saxa tuo.   10
non sinit Endymion te pectoris esse severi;
   flecte, precor, vultus ad mea furta tuos!
tu, dea, mortalem caelo delapsa petebas;
   vera loqui liceat!—quam sequor ipsa dea est.'

                        HEROIDES XVIII

mente agito, -are, -avi, -atum	I stir in my mind, remember
furtum, -i (n.)	secret mission
voluptas, -atis (f.)	pleasure
fores, -ium (f.pl.)	doors
lentus, -a, -um	(*here*) powerful
tremulus, -a, -um	shimmering
eunti	*supply* 'mihi'
officiosus, -a, -um	dutiful
suspicio, -ere, -spexi, -spectum	I look up at
Latmia saxa (n.pl.)	Mount Latmus (*where Endymion and Luna met*)
flecto, -ere, flexi, flexum	I turn, bend

DISCENDUM *Jussive and hortative subjunctives*

The present subjunctive is often used on its own to give a command (e.g. 'let justice be done' – jussive subjunctive) or encouragement ('let us rejoice' – hortative subjunctive). These are even more common in verse than in prose, and in fact there are three jussive subjunctives in this passage (*faveas; subeant; liceat*). Ensure you know your subjunctive endings thoroughly and look out for these.

Elegiac Passage 9 *Hero's dream*

Leander continues to visit his beloved Hero. But in this passage, Hero describes a dream in which she sees a dolphin washed up dead on the shore, and tells of her fear as to what this dream might portend.

Beware of swimming, Leander! The seas are rough and
dangerous. But still I want you to come to me.

sed mihi, <u>caeruleas</u> quotiens <u>obvertor</u> ad undas,
    nescio quid pavidum frigore pectus habet.
nec minus hesternae <u>confundor</u> imagine noctis,
    quamvis est sacris illa <u>piata</u> meis.
hic ego ventosas nantem <u>delphina</u> per undas   5
    cernere non dubia sum mihi visa fide:
quem postquam <u>bibulis</u> <u>illisit</u> <u>fluctus</u> harenis,
    unda simul miserum vitaque deseruit.
quidquid id est, timeo; nec tu mea somnia ride
    nec nisi <u>tranquillo</u> bracchia crede mari.   10
si tibi non parcis, dilectae parce puellae,
    quae numquam nisi te <u>sospite</u> <u>sospes</u> ero.
interea, quoniam nanti freta <u>pervia</u> non sunt,
    <u>leniat</u> invisas littera missa moras.

                         HEROIDES XIX

caeruleus, -a, -um	dark blue
obvertor, -i, -versus sum	I turn myself
confundor, -i, -fusus sum	I am in turmoil
pio, -are, -avi, -atum	I placate, appease
delphin, -inis (Gk acc. *-ina*) (m.)	dolphin
bibulus, -a, -um	thirsty
illido, -ere, -lisi, -lisum	I dash against
fluctus, -us (m.)	wave
tranquillus, -a, -um	calm
sospes, -itis	safe
pervius, -a, -um	crossable
lenio, -ire, -ivi, -itum	I soothe

DISCENDUM *Split passive forms*

Notice how, in verse, the two parts of perfect passive verbs are often separated and scattered across the line. While in prose *visa sum* is easily translated as 'I seem', it is rather trickier when we have <u>sum</u> *mihi* <u>visa</u> (line 6). Beware of this very common occurrence – in fact, it has also happened in line 4 with *est . . . piata*.

Elegiac Passage 10 *Ovid's afternoon of passion*

Ovid describes a steamy summer afternoon with his lover Corinna.

*As I was relaxing one sunny afternoon, in came Corinna, wearing a little dress
tied in the middle and with her hair falling over her white neck.*

deripui tunicam—nec multum rara nocebat;
    pugnabat tunica sed tamen illa tegi.
quae cum ita pugnaret, tamquam quae vincere nollet,
    victa est non aegre proditione sua.
ut stetit ante oculos posito velamine nostros,   5
    in toto nusquam corpore menda fuit.
quos umeros, quales vidi tetigique lacertos!
    forma papillarum quam fuit apta premi!
quam castigato planus sub pectore venter!
    quantum et quale latus! quam iuvenale femur!   10
singula quid referam? nil non laudabile vidi
    et nudam pressi corpus ad usque meum.
cetera quis nescit? lassi requievimus ambo.
    proveniant medii sic mihi saepe dies!

                                      AMORES I

rarus, -a, -um	skimpy (*here refers to the dress*)
tamquam quae . . .	like someone who . . .
proditio, -onis (f.)	surrender, betrayal
velamen, -inis (n.)	covering, clothes
menda, -ae (f.)	mark, blemish
papilla, -ae (f.)	breast
castigatus, -a, -um	slender
planus, -a, -um	flat
venter, -tris (m.)	stomach
femur, -oris (n.)	thigh
requiesco, -ere, -quievi, -quietum	I rest
ambo, -ae, -a	both

DISCENDUM *Using scansion*

You may have tried some scanning by now, but you may not have realized
how helpful it can be. Scanning line 2 will show the *-a* of *tunica* to be long
(*-ā*), meaning that it must be ablative (here, 'with the dress'); whereas the *-a*
of *illa* is short (*-ă*), and so must be nominative (feminine, referring to the
girl). So we know the translation must not be 'that dress . . .' (they cannot
agree), but rather 'she . . . with the dress'.

Elegiac Passage 11 *Have two girls on the go*

Ovid advises his lovesick reader to lessen the pains of love by dividing them: if
you have two girls, you feel half the agony. And if you need help finding another
girl, Ovid can also help . . .

I've given you my thoughts on sex. Now another tip:

hortor et ut pariter <u>binas</u> habeatis amicas
    (fortior est, plures siquis habere potest):
<u>grandia</u> per multos <u>tenuantur</u> flumina rivos,
    saevaque <u>diducto</u> <u>stipite</u> flamma perit.
non satis una tenet <u>ceratas</u> ancora puppes,   5
    nec satis est liquidis <u>unicus</u> <u>hamus</u> aquis.
<u>qui</u> sibi iam <u>pridem</u> <u>solacia</u> <u>bina</u> paravit,
    iam <u>pridem</u> summa victor in arce fuit.
at tibi, qui fueris dominae <u>male</u> creditus uni,
    nunc <u>saltem</u> novus est inveniendus amor.   10
quaeris, ubi invenias? artes tu <u>perlege</u> nostras:
    plena puellarum iam tibi navis erit.

                      REMEDIA AMORIS

bini, -ae, -a	two
grandis, -e	large
tenuo, -are, -avi, -atum	I make thin, thin out
diduco, -ere, -duxi, -ductum	I separate
stipes, -itis (m.)	log
ceratus, -a, -um	waxed, wax-covered
unicus, -a, -um	a single
hamus, -i (m.)	fishing hook
qui	'he who . . .'
pridem	long ago
solacium, -ii (n.)	consolation
male	(*here*) mistakenly
saltem	at least
perlego, -ere, -lexi, -lectum	I read thoroughly

DISCENDUM *The royal 'we'*

Ovid often uses plural nouns when the singular is meant. This poetic plural
for singular occurs especially commonly with words for 'we', 'us', 'our', etc.,
which are used as a sort of royal we to mean just 'I', 'my', etc. Look at line 11
here: what does Ovid really mean by *artes . . . nostras*?

Elegiac Passage 12 *Ovid's book arrives in Rome*

Ovid's book comes to Rome from Tomis and asks a friendly stranger to show it around the great buildings, including Augustus' house itself.

'Tell me,' I asked, 'where I, a book from a foreign land, should go in this city of Rome.' And at last I found someone to help me, and said:

'duc, age! namque sequar, quamvis terraque marique
    longinquo referam lassus ab orbe pedem.'
paruit, et ducens 'haec sunt fora Caesaris,' inquit,
    'haec est a sacris quae via nomen habet,
hic locus est Vestae, qui Pallada servat et ignem,   5
    haec fuit antiqui regia parva Numae.'
inde petens dextram 'porta est' ait 'ista Palati,
    hic Stator, hoc primum condita Roma loco est.'
singula dum miror, video fulgentibus armis
    conspicuos postes tectaque digna deo.   10
'et Iovis haec' dixi 'domus est?' quod ut esse putarem,
    augurium menti querna corona dabat.
cuius ut accepi dominum, 'non fallimur,' inquam,
    'et magni verum est hanc Iovis esse domum.'

                    TRISTIA III

age!	come now!
longinquus, -a, -um	far-off
Vesta, -ae (f.)	Vesta (*goddess of the hearth*)
Numa, -ae (m.)	Numa (*second king of Rome*)
Palatium, -i (n.)	Palatine Hill
Stator, -oris (m.)	'the Stayer' (*a title of Jupiter*)
postis, -is (m.)	gate post
quod ut esse putarem	'for me to think this'
augurium, -ii (n.)	sign, indication
quernus, -a, -um	of oak leaf
accipio, -ere, -cepi, -ceptum	(*here*) I hear, learn

DISCENDUM *Conjunctions out of place*

Look out for conjunctions (*et, sed, ut, cum*, etc.) or the relative pronoun (*qui, quae, quod*) out of position. The delayed *dum* in line 9 should be manageable, but look at line 4: for *haec est a sacris quae* you might be thinking 'this is from the sacred rites which ...'. But in fact the *quae* is again in an awkward position: the translation only works as, 'this is the road which ...'. Do be alert to this very nasty phenomenon.

Elegiac Passage 13　*Ovid's dreams in exile*

Ovid is lamenting his lot in exile. He dreams sometimes that he is being attacked by the Sarmatians, or sometimes that he is back in Rome again.

Sleep provides me with some respite from my troubles, though even there dreams frighten me and take me back to my waking anxieties.

at, puto, cum requies medicinaque publica curae
　　somnus adest, solitis nox venit orba malis.
somnia me terrent veros imitantia casus
　　et vigilant sensus in mea damna mei.
aut ego Sarmaticas videor vitare sagittas　　　　　　　5
　　aut dare captivas ad fera vincla manus
aut, ubi decipior melioris imagine somni,
　　aspicio patriae tecta relicta meae.
et modo vobiscum, quos sum veneratus, amici,
　　et modo cum cara coniuge multa loquor.　　　　　10
sive dies igitur caput hoc miserabile cernit,
　　sive pruinosi noctis aguntur equi,
sic mea perpetuis liquefiunt pectora curis,
　　ignibus admotis ut nova cera solet.

　　　　　　　　　　　　　　　　　EX PONTO I

medicina, -ae (f.)	remedy
publicus, -a, -um	(*here*) common
orbus, -a, -um (+ abl.)	(*here*) free from
imitor, -ari, -atus sum	I resemble
casus, -us (m.)	event, calamity
vigilo, -are, -avi, -atum	I am awake
damnum, -i (n.)	(*here*) misfortune
Sarmaticus, -a, -um	of the Sarmatians (*a local tribe*)
veneror, -ari, -atus sum	I honour, revere
pruinosus, -a, -um	frosty
perpetuus, -a, -um	continuous
liquefio, -fieri, -factus sum	I melt
cera, -ae (f.)	wax

DISCENDUM　*Translating 'ut'*

The use of *ut* in line 14 here is a good reminder of how tricky this word can be in verse. First, remember that with the indicative it does not mean 'in order to', etc., but simply 'as' or 'when'. Second, remember that, like other conjunctions, it can be delayed from the beginning of the clause, where you will be used to seeing it in prose.

Elegiac Passage 14 *Protesilaus departs*

Laodamia tells her husband Protesilaus how she watched intently the sails of his
ship as he departed to the Trojan War, and then she fainted.

*The winds were good for your sailors, but not for me. Once we had embraced, I
scarcely had time to say 'goodbye' before you were off.*

incubuit Boreas abreptaque vela tetendit,
  iamque meus longe Protesilaus erat.
dum potui spectare virum, spectare placebat,
  sumque tuos oculos usque secuta meis;
si te non poteram, poteram tua vela videre,   5
  vela diu vultus detinuere meos.
at postquam nec te nec vela fugacia vidi,
  et quod spectarem, nil nisi pontus erat,
mens quoque tecum abiit, tenebrisque exsanguis obortis
  succiduo dicor procubuisse genu.   10
vix socer Iphiclus, vix me grandaevus Acastus,
  vix mater gelida maesta refecit aqua.
ut rediit animus, pariter rediere dolores;
  pectora legitimus casta momordit amor.

                                    HEROIDES XIII

incumbo, -ere, -cubui, -cubitum	I swoop down
vultus, -us, (m.)	(*here*) gaze
fugax, -acis	fleeing
exsanguis, -e	faint, pale
oborior, -iri, -ortus sum	I rise up
succiduus, -a, -um	bended
procumbo, -ere, -cubui, -cubitum	I fall forwards
socer, -eri (m.)	father-in-law
Iphiclus, -i (m.)	Iphiclus (*Protesilaus' father*)
grandaevus, -a, -um	aged, old
Acastus, -i (m.)	Acastus (*Laodamia's father*)
mordeo, -ere, momordi, morsum	I bite

DISCENDUM *Poetic plural for singular*

Poetry often uses a plural noun when the singular is meant. The only way
to tell is by the sense of the sentence – in line 6, *meos . . . vultus* is plural (lit.
'my faces'), but this sounds too odd in English and so we should translate
it just as a singular.

Elegiac Passage 15 *The judgment of Paris*

Paris tells how Mercury appeared to him with three goddesses (Venus, Pallas Athene
and Juno) and ordered him to judge who was the most beautiful of the three.

There is a lovely grove in the valleys of Mount Ida
where no animals ever come to graze.

hinc ego <u>Dardaniae</u> muros <u>excelsa</u>que tecta
   et freta prospiciens arbore nixus eram—
ecce, pedum <u>pulsu</u> visa est mihi terra moveri—
   vera loquar veri vix habitura fidem—
constitit ante oculos actus velocibus alis   5
   <u>Atlantis</u> magni <u>Pleiones</u>que <u>nepos</u>,
tresque simul divae, Venus et cum Pallade Iuno,
   <u>graminibus</u> teneros imposuere pedes.
<u>obstupui</u>, gelidusque comas <u>erexerat</u> horror,
   cum mihi 'pone metum!' nuntius ales ait: 10
'<u>arbiter</u> es formae. certamina <u>siste</u> dearum:
   vincere quae forma digna sit una duas.'
vincere erant omnes dignae iudexque querebar
   non omnes causam vincere posse suam.

                      HEROIDES XVI

Dardania, -ae (f.)	Troy
excelsus, -a, -um	high
pulsus, -us (m.)	beat, tread
Atlas, -antis (m.)	Atlas (*Mercury's grandfather*)
Pleione, -es (Gk decl.) (f.)	Pleione (*Mercury's grandmother*)
nepos, -otis (m.)	grandson
gramen, -inis (n.)	grass
obstupesco, -ere, -pui	I am stunned
erigo, -ere, -rexi, -rectum	I make *x* to stand on end
arbiter, -tri (m.)	judge
sisto, -ere, stiti, statum	I stop

DISCENDUM *Declension clashes*

There is a danger of falling into the lazy habit of piecing words together by
rhyme alone (e.g. *excelsa tecta* in line 1 or *forma digna* in line 12). This
approach will fail when dealing with words of different declensions; care is
needed to see that *teneros* (2nd decl.) and *pedes* (3rd decl.) agree, or *nuntius*
… *ales* or *gelidus* … *horror*.

Elegiac Passage 16 *Pan and the Luperci*

At the Roman festival of the Lupercalia, two youths were selected to be the *Luperci* and to run about naked except for belts of goatskin. Ovid explains that this tradition comes from the god Pan and his followers, who used to do this long before the birth of Jupiter and even before the birth of the Moon.

Pan is an ancient deity, whom we still worship: we hold the 'Lupercalia' in his honour, where his devotees, the 'Luperci', run about naked.

cur igitur currant, et cur (sic currere mos est)
    nuda ferant posita corpora veste, rogas?
ipse deus velox discurrere gaudet in altis
    montibus, et subitas <u>concipit</u> ipse fugas:
ipse deus nudus nudos iubet ire ministros;   5
    nec satis ad cursus <u>commoda</u> vestis erit.
ante Iovem genitum terras habuisse <u>feruntur</u>
    <u>Arcades</u>, et luna gens prior illa fuit.
nullus <u>anhelabat</u> sub <u>adunco</u> vomere taurus,
    nulla sub imperio terra <u>colentis</u> erat: 10
nullus adhuc erat usus equi; se quisque ferebat:
    ibat ovis <u>lana</u> corpus <u>amicta</u> sua.
<u>sub Iove</u> <u>durabant</u> et corpora nuda gerebant,
    docta graves imbres et tolerare Notos.

                          FASTI II

concipio, -ere, -cepi, -ceptum	(*here*) I instigate
commodus, -a, -um	convenient
feruntur	(they) are said
Arcades, -um (m.pl.)	Arcadians (*inhabitants of Arcadia in Greece, home of Pan*)
anhelo, -are, -avi, -atum	I pant
aduncus, -a, -um	hooked
colens, -entis (m.)	farmer
lana, -ae (f.)	wool
amictus, -a, -um	clad in, clothed in
sub Iove	in the open air
duro, -are, -avi, -atum	I harden, toughen up

BONUS

1. Try scanning lines 3–4.
2. In lines 9–14, how does Ovid's language evoke the hardy simplicity of ancient Arcadia? Try to make **three** points.

Elegiac Passage 17 *Only a prostitute sells herself*

Ovid tells how he lost all desire for his girl once she began to demand a price for her love.

I used to be so in love with you that I feared every animal
might be Jupiter in disguise, seeking your affection.

nunc timor omnis abest, animique <u>resanuit</u> error,
    nec facies oculos iam capit ista meos.
cur sim mutatus, quaeris? quia munera poscis.
    haec te non <u>patitur</u> causa placere mihi.
<u>donec</u> eras simplex, animum cum corpore amavi;   5
    nunc mentis <u>vitio</u> laesa figura tua est.
et puer est et nudus Amor; sine <u>sordibus</u> annos
    et nullas vestes, ut sit apertus, habet.
quid puerum Veneris pretio <u>prostare</u> iubetis?
    quo pretium <u>condat</u>, non habet ille <u>sinum</u>!   10
nec Venus apta feris Veneris nec filius armis—
    non decet <u>imbelles</u> <u>aera merere</u> deos.
stat <u>meretrix</u> certo <u>cuivis</u> <u>mercabilis</u> <u>aere</u>,
    et, quod vos facitis sponte, coacta facit.

                           AMORES I

resanesco, -ere, -nui	I heal again
patior, -i, passus sum	(*here*) I allow
donec	as long as
vitium, -ii (n.)	fault
sordes, -ium (f.pl.)	disgrace, filth
prosto, -are, -stiti, -statum	I prostitute myself
condo, -ere, -didi, -ditum	(*here*) I keep, store
sinus, -us (m.)	(*here*) pocket
imbellis, -e	unwarlike
aera mereo, -ere, -ui, -itum	I draw a soldier's pay
meretrix, -icis (f.)	prostitute
cuivis	'to anyone at all'
mercabilis, -e	on sale
aes, aeris (n.)	(*here*) fee

BONUS

1. Try scanning lines 3–4.
2. In lines 7–12, how does Ovid's language convey disgust at his girl's inappropriate conduct? Try to make **three** points.

Elegiac Passage 18 *Ovid's ordeals in exile*

In exile on the Black Sea, Ovid complains about the weather, the people and the
dangers in his new country.

The poem begins:

> ut sumus in Ponto, ter frigore constitit Hister,
>   facta est Euxini dura ter unda maris.
> at mihi iam videor patria procul esse tot annis,
>   Dardana quot Graio Troia sub hoste fuit.
> innumerae circa gentes fera bella minantur,   5
>   quae sibi non rapto vivere turpe putant.
> nil extra tutum est: tumulus defenditur ipse
>   moenibus exiguis ingenioque loci.
> cum minime credas, ut aves, densissimus hostis
>   advolat, et praedam vix bene visus agit.   10
> est igitur rarus, rus qui colere audeat, isque
>   hac arat infelix, hac tenet arma manu.

TRISTIA V

Pontus, -i (m.)	Pontus (*the province by the Black Sea to which Ovid has been exiled*)
Hister, -tri (m.)	River Danube
Euxinus, -a, -um	of the Black Sea
Dardanus, -a, -um	Dardanian (*of Dardanus, the founder of Troy*)
Graius, -a, -um	Greek
raptum, -i (n.)	pillage, theft
tumulus, -i (m.)	mound, hill
ingenium, -ii (n.)	(*here*) nature
advolo, -are, -avi, -atum	I fly towards
aro, -are, -avi, -atum	I plough

BONUS

1. Try scanning lines 5-6.
2. In lines 7-12, how does Ovid exaggerate the scale of his hardships?
   Try to make **three** points.

Elegiac Passage 19 *The death of Remus*

As Romulus begins to mark out the boundaries of his new city, Rome, his brother
Remus ignores his warnings and meets with a violent end.

First Romulus established a holy place, filling a
trench with crops and erecting an altar on top.

inde premens <u>stivam</u> designat moenia <u>sulco</u>;
    alba iugum niveo cum bove vacca tulit.
ille precabatur, <u>tonitru</u> dedit <u>omina</u> <u>laevo</u>
    Iuppiter, et <u>laevo</u> fulmina missa polo.
<u>augurio</u> laeti iaciunt <u>fundamina</u> cives,   5
    et novus exiguo tempore murus erat.
hoc <u>Celer</u> urget opus, quem Romulus ipse vocarat,
    'sint,' que, '<u>Celer</u>, curae' dixerat 'ista tuae,
neve quis aut muros aut factam vomere fossam
    transeat; audentem talia dede <u>neci</u>.'   10
quod Remus ignorans <u>humiles</u> <u>contemnere</u> muros
    coepit, et 'his populus' dicere 'tutus erit?'
nec mora, transiluit: <u>rutro</u> <u>Celer</u> <u>occupat</u> ausum;
    ille premit duram <u>sanguinulentus</u> humum.

                            FASTI IV

stiva, -ae (f.)	plough handle
sulcus, -i (m.)	ditch, furrow
tonitrus, -us (m.)	thunder
omen, -inis (n.)	omen
laevus, -a, -um	on the left
augurium, -ii (n.)	omen
fundamen, -inis (n.)	foundation
Celer, -eri (m.)	Celer (*an officer of Romulus*)
nex, necis (f.)	death
humilis, -e	low
contemno, -ere, -psi, -ptum	I disparage, mock
rutrum, -i (n.)	spade
occupo, -are, -avi, -atum	(*here*) I hit
sanguinulentus, -a, -um	pouring out blood

BONUS

1. Try scanning lines 3–4.
2. In lines 9–14, how does Ovid's language make his story dramatic? Try
    to make **three** points.

Elegiac Passage 20 *Ovid craves gossip from Rome*

Stuck in exile in Tomis, Ovid hopes that spring will bring him more news from
Rome as the seas become navigable again.

Now I feel that spring is on the way and snow and ice
are starting to melt.

nec mare <u>concrescit</u> glacie, nec, ut ante, per <u>Histrum</u>
   <u>stridula</u> <u>Sauromates</u> <u>plaustra</u> <u>bubulcus</u> agit.
rarus ab Italia tantum mare navita transit,
   litora rarus in haec portibus <u>orba</u> venit.
sive tamen Graeca scierit, sive ille Latina   5
   voce loqui (certe gratior <u>huius</u> erit),
quisquis is est, <u>memori</u> rumorem voce referre
   et fieri famae parsque gradusque potest.
is, precor, auditos possit narrare triumphos
   <u>Caesaris</u> et <u>Latio</u> reddita vota Iovi,   10
teque, <u>rebellatrix</u>, tandem, <u>Germania</u>, magni
   triste caput pedibus supposuisse ducis.
haec mihi qui referet, quae non vidisse dolebo,
   ille meae domui protinus hospes erit.

                             TRISTIA III

concresco, -ere, -crevi, -cretum	I am frozen hard
Hister, -tri (m.)	River Danube
stridulus, -a, -um	rattling
Sauromates, -is	Sarmatian (*a local tribe*)
plaustrum, -i (n.)	cart
bubulcus, -i (m.)	herdsman
orbus, -a, -um (+ abl.)	lacking, without
hic, haec, hoc	(*here*) the latter (*i.e. Latin*)
memor, -oris	remembering
Caesar, -aris (m.)	Augustus Caesar
Latius, -a, -um	Latin
rebellatrix, -icis	rebellious
Germania, -ae (f.)	Germany

BONUS

1. Try scanning lines 13–14.
2. In lines 7–12, how does Ovid's language bring out his excitement at
    the possibility of hearing news from Rome? Try to make **three** points.

Elegiac Passage 21 *Ovid hopes to be buried in Italy*

In the misery of exile, Ovid contemplates his death. He tells his wife that he will not be buried at home in Italy, but he prays that death might at last bring total deliverance from the horrible place he now inhabits.

I should happily have died when I should have been buried
at home. But instead I was given life so I could die an exile.

tam procul ignotis igitur moriemur in oris,
    et fient ipso tristia fata loco;
nec mandata dabo, nec cum clamore supremo
    labentes oculos condet amica manus;
sed sine funeribus caput hoc, sine honore sepulcri   5
    indeploratum barbara terra teget.
ecquid, ubi audieris, tota turbabere mente,
    et feries pavida pectora fida manu?
ecquid, in has frustra tendens tua bracchia partes,
    clamabis miseri nomen inane viri?   10
parce tamen lacerare genas, nec scinde capillos:
    non tibi nunc primum, lux mea, raptus ero.
cum patriam amisi, tunc me periisse putato:
    et prior et gravior mors fuit illa mihi.
atque utinam pereant animae cum corpore nostrae,   15
    effugiatque avidos pars mihi nulla rogos!
nam si morte carens vacua volat altus in aura
    spiritus, et Samii sunt rata dicta senis,[1]
inter Sarmaticas Romana vagabitur umbras,
    perque feros manes hospita semper erit.   20
ossa tamen facito parva referantur in urna:
    sic ego non etiam mortuus exul ero.

                                      TRISTIA III

mandatum, -i (n.)	(*here*) last wishes
condo, -ere, -didi, -ditum	(*here*) I close
sepulcrum, -i (n.)	tomb
indeploratus, -a, -um	unlamented
ecquid	*introduces a question*

---

[1]   This refers to Pythagoras, a philosopher from Samos who believed in the reincarnation of the soul after death.

turbo, -are, -avi, -atum	I throw into confusion
parce (+ infin.)	don't
scindo, -ere, scidi, scissum	I cut
putato (future imperative)	let it be thought ...
avidus, -a, -um	all-consuming
Samius, -a, -um	of Samos (*a Greek island*)
ratus, -a, -um	true, valid
Sarmaticus, -a, -um	Sarmatian (*a tribe in Tomis, where Ovid is in exile*)
vagor, -ari, -atus sum	I wander
hospita, -ae (f.)	stranger
os, ossis (n.)	bone
facito (future imperative)	make sure that ...

(a) Translate lines 1–10 (*tam ... viri*) into good English. **Please write your translation on alternate lines.**   [30]

(b) Lines 11–12 (*parce ... ero*):

   (i)   what **two** things does Ovid forbid his wife to do if he should die?   [2]

   (ii)   what does he say to comfort her about his death?   [1]

   (iii) write out and scan these lines.   [4]

(c) In lines 13–14 (*cum ... mihi*), explain the point Ovid is making about his exile.   [2]

(d) In lines 15–16 (*atque ... rogos*), what does Ovid hope will happen to him when he dies?   [1]

(e) Looking at lines 19–20 (*inter ... erit*), why does Ovid not want to survive death at all?   [2]

(f) In lines 15–20 (*atque ... erit*), how does Ovid's use of language emphasize his fear about his fate after death? Make **three** points and refer to the Latin.   [6]

(g) In lines 21–22 (*ossa ... ero*), what last request does Ovid make for his remains, and why does he want this?   [2]

Total [50]

Elegiac Passage 22 *A triumphant lover*

Having won the attentions of his beloved Corinna, Ovid thinks he deserves a great triumph to celebrate.

The poem begins:

ite triumphales circum mea tempora laurus!
   vicimus: in nostro est, ecce, Corinna sinu,
quam vir, quam custos, quam ianua firma, tot hostes,
   servabant, nequa posset ab arte capi!
haec est praecipuo victoria digna triumpho,   5
   in qua, quaecumque est, sanguine praeda caret.
non humiles muri, non parvis oppida fossis
   cincta, sed est ductu capta puella meo!
me duce ad hanc voti finem, me milite veni;
   ipse eques, ipse pedes, signifer ipse fui.   10
nec belli est nova causa mei. nisi rapta fuisset
   Tyndaris, Europae pax Asiaeque foret.
femina Troianos iterum nova bella movere
   impulit in regno, iuste Latine, tuo;
femina Romanis etiamnunc urbe recenti   15
   immisit soceros armaque saeva dedit.[1]
vidi ego pro nivea pugnantes coniuge tauros;
   spectatrix animos ipsa iuvenca dabat.
me quoque, qui multos, sed me sine caede, Cupido
   iussit militiae signa movere suae.   20
                              AMORES II

triumphalis, -e	triumphal, of a triumph
tempora, -um (n.pl.)	temples (*of the head*)
laurus, -us (f.)	laurel
praecipuus, -a, -um	exceptional
humilis, -e	low
fossa, -ae (f.)	trench
signifer, -eri (m.)	standard-bearer
Tyndaris, -idis (f.)	daughter of Tyndareus (= *Helen of Troy*)

[1]   Ovid is referring to the rape of the Sabine women: when the early Romans stole the womenfolk of the Sabines, a neighbouring tribe, the girls' angry fathers attacked Rome (see Passages 3 and 4).

Latinus, -i (m.)	Latinus (*an Italian king*)
etiamnunc	still, yet (*with* 'recenti')
socer, -eri (m.)	father-in-law
iuvenca, -ae (f.)	heifer, young cow

(a) In lines 1–2 (*ite . . . sinu*), what exactly does Ovid order to happen, and why?   [1+1]

(b) In lines 1–4 (*ite . . . capi*), how does Ovid's language glorify his conquest? Make **two** points and refer to the Latin.   [4]

(c) Lines 5–6 (*haec . . . caret*): how does Ovid rate his own victory, and why?   [2+2]

(d) Translate lines 7–16 (*non . . . dedit*) into good English. **Please write your translation on alternate lines.**   [30]

(e) Look at lines 17–18 (*vidi . . . dabat*):

   (i) what did Ovid see?   [2]

   (ii) how does this relate to the point Ovid is trying to make?   [2]

(f) What do you think Ovid means in line 20 by *militiae signa movere suae*?   [2]

(g) Write out and scan lines 19–20 (*me . . . suae*).   [4]

Total [50]

Elegiac Passage 23　*Ovid sees his lover cheating*

Ovid tells his beloved how he actually saw her being unfaithful at a dinner party, when she thought he was asleep.

The poem begins:

nullus amor tanti est—abeas, pharetrate Cupido!—
　ut mihi sint totiens maxima vota mori.
vota mori mea sunt, cum te peccasse recordor,
　o mihi perpetuum nata puella malum!
non male deletae nudant tua facta tabellae,　　　　　　　　5
　nec data furtive munera crimen habent.
o utinam arguerem sic, ut non vincere possem!
　me miserum! quare tam bona causa mea est?
felix, qui quod amat defendere fortiter audet,
　cui sua 'non feci!' dicere amica potest.　　　　　　　　10
ipse miser vidi, cum me dormire putares,
　sobrius adposito crimina vestra mero.
multa supercilio vidi vibrante loquentes;
　nutibus in vestris pars bona vocis erat.
non oculi tacuere tui, conscriptaque vino　　　　　　　　15
　mensa, nec in digitis littera nulla fuit.
iamque frequens ierat mensa conviva relicta;
　compositi iuvenes unus et alter erant.
improba tum vero iungentes oscula vidi—
　illa mihi lingua nexa fuisse liquet—　　　　　　　　20
qualia non fratri tulerit germana severo,
　sed tulerit cupido mollis amica viro.

　　　　　　　　　　　　　　　　　　AMORES II

tanti est	is worth so much
pharetratus, -a, -um	quiver-wearing
pecco, -are, -avi, -atum	I sin, offend
recordor, -ari, -atus sum	I remember
male deletus, -a, -um	partly rubbed out
nudo, -are, -avi, -atum	(*here*) I make clear, reveal
tabella, -ae (f.)	wax tablet
arguo, -ere, -ui, -utum	I make an accusation
sobrius, -a, -um	sober
adpono, -ere, -posui, -positum	(*here*) I lay aside
merum, -i (n.)	wine

supercilium, -ii (n.)	brow
nutus, -us (m.)	nod
frequens, -entis	crowds of
conviva, -ae (m.)	dinner guest (*take as pl.*)
compositus, -a, -um	(*here*) laid out
unus et alter	a few
necto, -ere, nexui, nexum	I entwine
liqueo, -ere, licui	I am clear, evident

(**a**) Write out and scan lines 1–2 (*nullus . . . mori*). [4]

(**b**) Look at lines 1–4 (*nullus . . . malum*):

    (**i**)   for what does Ovid pray? [1]

    (**ii**) when does he make this prayer? [1]

    (**iii**) how, by the style and content of these lines, does Ovid convey his desire to be free from his love? Make **two** points and refer to the Latin. [4]

(**c**) Lines 5–6 (*non male . . . habent*): in which **two** ways does Ovid say that he did **not** find out about his beloved's infidelity? [2]

(**d**) Lines 7–8 (*o utinam . . . mea est*): considering what follows, explain the point Ovid is making here, in your own words. [2]

(**e**) Translate lines 9–18 (*felix . . . erant*) into good English. **Please write your translation on alternate lines.** [30]

(**f**) In lines 19–20 (*improba . . . liquet*), how did Ovid know that these were the kisses of lovers? [2]

(**g**) In lines 19–22 (*improba . . . viro*), how does Ovid, by his choice of words and other stylistic features, present his beloved's behaviour as especially outrageous? Make **two** points and refer to the Latin in your answer. [4]

Total [50]

Elegiac Passage 24 *Ariadne loses Theseus I*

Ariadne has been abandoned on the island of Naxos by her one-time lover, the
hero Theseus. Here she writes to him, describing the moment when she realized
he had left her.

The poem begins:

> illa relicta feris etiam nunc, improbe Theseu,
>   vivit. et haec aequa mente tulisse velis?
> quae legis, ex illo, Theseu, tibi litore mitto
>   unde tuam sine me vela tulere ratem,
> in quo me somnusque meus male prodidit et tu,   5
>   per facinus somnis insidiate meis.
> tempus erat, vitrea quo primum terra pruina
>   spargitur et tectae fronde queruntur aves;
> incertum vigilans ac somno languida movi
>   Thesea prensuras semisupina manus: 10
> nullus erat. referoque manus iterumque retempto
>   perque torum moveo bracchia: nullus erat.
> excussere metus somnum; conterrita surgo
>   membraque sunt viduo praecipitata toro.
> protinus adductis sonuerunt pectora palmis   15
>   utque erat e somno turbida, rupta coma est.
> luna fuit; specto si quid nisi litora cernam;
>   quod videant oculi, nil nisi litus habent.
> nunc huc, nunc illuc et utroque sine ordine, curro,
>   alta puellares tardat harena pedes.   20
> interea toto clamanti litore 'Theseu!'
>   reddebant nomen concava saxa tuum
> et quotiens ego te, totiens locus ipse vocabat;
>   ipse locus miserae ferre volebat opem.
>   HEROIDES X

Theseus (Gk voc. *-eu*; acc. *-ea*) (m.)	Theseus
insidior, -ari, -atus sum	I plot
vitreus, -a, -um	like glass, glassy
pruina, -ae (f.)	frost
incertum	uncertainly
vigilo, -are, -avi, -atum	I am awake
languidus, -a, -um	sluggish
prendo, -ere, -di, -sum	I lay hold of, grasp

semisupinus, -a, -um	half turning, on one's side
retempto, -are, -avi, -atum	I try again
membrum, -i (n.)	limb
praecipito, -are, -avi, -atum	I throw wildly
adduco, -ere, -duxi, -ductum	(*here*) I thump against
turbidus, -a, -um	in disarray
utroque	in both directions
tardo, -are, -avi, -atum	I slow, hinder
concavus, -a, -um	arched, curved

(a) Translate lines 1–11 (*illa relicta . . . nullus erat*) into good English. **Please write your translation on alternate lines.** [30]

(b) Look at lines 9–12 (*incertum . . . nullus erat*):

    (i) Write out and scan lines 11–12. [4]

    (ii) In lines 9–12, how do the style and rhythm of the words make Ariadne's discovery as she awakes dramatic? Make **three** points and refer to the Latin. [6]

(c) From lines 13–14 (*excussere . . . toro*), pick out and translate **two** words which indicate Ariadne's mental state. [2]

(d) Lines 15–16 (*protinus . . . coma est*): in what **two** ways did Ariadne show her grief? [2]

(e) In lines 17–18 (*luna . . . habent*), what did Ariadne see? [1]

(f) Look at lines 19–24 (*nunc . . . opem*):

    (i) how does Ovid's language convey Ariadne's desperation? Make **two** points and refer to the Latin. [4]

    (ii) what does Ariadne mean by her comment in line 24? [1]

Total [50]

Elegiac Passage 25 *Ariadne loses Theseus II*

The abandoned Ariadne tells how she climbed a mountain and looked for
Theseus' ship on the sea below, describing her grief as she watched him sail away.

There I saw a hill with bushes on its summit
and a cliff overhanging the waves.

ascendo; vires animus dabat; atque ita late
  aequora prospectu <u>metior</u> alta meo.
inde ego—nam ventis quoque <u>sum</u> crudelibus <u>usa</u>—
  vidi praecipiti <u>carbasa</u> tenta Noto.
ut vidi haud dignam quae me vidisse putarem,   5
  frigidior glacie semianimisque fui.
nec <u>languere</u> diu patitur dolor. excitor illo,
  excitor et summa <u>Thesea</u> voce voco.
'quo fugis?' exclamo '<u>scelerate</u> revertere <u>Theseu</u>!
  flecte ratem! numerum non habet illa suum!'   10
haec ego. quod voci <u>deerat</u>, <u>plangore</u> replebam;
  <u>verbera</u> cum verbis mixta fuere meis.
si non audires, ut <u>saltem</u> cernere posses,
  iactatae late signa dedere manus.
iamque oculis ereptus eras. tum denique flevi;   15
  <u>torpuerant</u> molles ante dolore genae.
quid potius facerent, quam <u>me</u> mea lumina <u>flerent</u>,
  postquam desieram vela videre tua?
aut ego diffusis erravi sola capillis,
  qualis ab <u>Ogygio</u> concita <u>Baccha</u> deo;   20
aut mare prospiciens in saxo frigida sedi,
  <u>quam</u>que <u>lapis</u> sedes, <u>tam</u> <u>lapis</u> ipsa fui.

                                                    HEROIDES X

metior, -iri, mensus sum	(*here*) I scan
utor, -i, usus sum (+ abl.)	(*here*) I experience
carbasa, -orum (n.pl.)	sails
langueo, -ere	I am inactive
Theseus (Gk voc. *-eu*; acc. *-ea*) (m.)	Theseus
sceleratus, -a, -um	wicked, accursed
desum, -esse, -fui (+ dat.)	I am lacking in
plangor, -oris (m.)	beating of one's breast
verber, -eris (n.)	blow, strike
saltem	at least

torpeo, -ere, -ui	I am numb
me . . . flerent	'weep for me'
Ogygius, -a, -um	Theban (*of Thebes, a city in Greece*)
Baccha, -ae (f.)	a Bacchante[1]
quam . . . tam . . .	just as . . . so . . .
lapis, -idis (m.)	rock

(a) Look at lines 1–2 (*ascendo . . . meo*):

    (i) what aided Ariadne as she climbed?   [1]

    (ii) what was she able to do from the top of the mountain?   [2]

(b) In lines 3–6 (*inde . . . fui*), how do Ariadne's words evoke her sense of horror at what she has seen? Make **two** points and refer to the style and content of the Latin.   [4]

(c) Look at lines 7–10 (*nec . . . ratem*):

    (i) what prevented Ariadne from being inactive?   [1]

    (ii) how does Ariadne's language here convey the depth of her emotions? Make **two** points and refer to the Latin.   [4]

(d) What do you think Ariadne means by *numerum non habet illa suum* (line 10)?   [2]

(e) In lines 11–12 (*haec . . . meis*), how does Ariadne encourage us to pity her?   [2]

(f) Translate lines 13–22 (*si . . . fui*) into good English. **Please write your translation on alternate lines.**   [30]

(g) Write out and scan lines 21–22 (*aut . . . fui*).   [4]

Total [50]

---

[1] The Bacchantes were female followers of the god of wine, Bacchus (Dionysus). They were famous for their wild religious orgies.

Elegiac Passage 26 *The destruction of the Fabii*

Ovid tells the story of one of Rome's most noble families. The Fabii were putting Rome's Etruscan enemies to flight all over the battlefield, until they were at last slaughtered to a man in an ambush.

As rumour has it, three hundred Fabii went
forth to battle through the gate of Carmentis.

ut <u>celeri passu</u> <u>Cremeram</u> tetigere <u>rapacem</u>
    (<u>turbidus hibernis</u> ille fluebat aquis),
castra loco ponunt: destrictis ensibus ipsi
    <u>Tyrrhenum</u> valido Marte per agmen eunt;
<u>non aliter quam</u> cum <u>Libyca</u> de gente leones   5
    invadunt sparsos lata per arva greges.
diffugiunt hostes <u>inhonesta</u>que vulnera tergo
    accipiunt: <u>Tusco</u> sanguine terra rubet.
sic iterum, sic saepe cadunt; ubi vincere aperte
    non <u>datur</u>, insidias armaque tecta parant.   10
in medio paucos armentaque rara relinquunt,
    cetera <u>virgultis</u> abdita turba latet.
ecce velut torrens undis <u>pluvialibus</u> auctus
    aut nive, quae Zephyro victa tepente fluit,
per <u>sata</u> perque vias fertur nec, ut ante solebat,   15
    riparum clausas <u>margine</u> <u>finit</u> aquas,
sic <u>Fabii</u> vallem latis <u>discursibus</u> implent,
    quodque vident sternunt, nec metus alter inest.
quo ruitis, <u>generosa</u> domus? male creditis hosti:
    simplex nobilitas, perfida tela cave!   20
fraude perit virtus: in apertos undique campos
    prosiliunt hostes et latus omne tenent.
una dies <u>Fabios</u> ad bellum miserat omnes,
    ad bellum missos perdidit una dies.

                                FASTI II

celeri passu	quickly, at a quick pace
Cremera, -ae (f.)	Cremera (*a river in Italy*)
rapax, -acis	(*here*) rushing
turbidus, -a, -um	swollen, swirling
hibernus, -a, -um	of winter
Tyrrhenus, -a, -um	Etruscan
non aliter quam	just as

Libycus, -a, -um	of Libya, Libyan
inhonestus, -a, -um	dishonourable
Tuscus, -a, -um	Etruscan
datur (impers.)	it was granted, allowed
virgulta, -orum (n.pl.)	thicket
pluvialis, -e	of rain
sata, -orum (n.pl.)	crops
margo, -inis (m.)	edge, boundary
finio, -ire, -ivi, -itum	I enclose, contain
Fabii, -orum (m.pl.)	the Fabii (*a Roman family*)
discursus, -us (m.)	running to and fro
generosus, -a, -um	noble

(a) Translate lines 1–10 (*ut . . . parant*) into good English. **Please write your translation on alternate lines.** [30]

(b) Write out and scan lines 11–12 (*in medio . . . latet*). [4]

(c) Looking at lines 11–12 (*in medio . . . latet*), describe how the ambush was set. [2]

(d) Lines 13–16 (*ecce . . . aquas*): how does Ovid, by his choice and position of words, make this simile powerful and effective? Make **two** points and refer to the Latin. [4]

(e) Look at lines 17–18 (*sic . . . inest*):

  (i) what do the Fabii do here? Answer in detail. [3]

  (ii) what does Ovid say about the Fabii's courage? [1]

(f) In lines 19–24 (*quo . . . dies*), how does Ovid make the ambush on the Fabii and their deaths dramatic and pitiable? Make **three** points and refer to the Latin. [6]

Total [50]

Elegiac Passage 27 *Find another victim, Cupid!*

Ovid reproaches Cupid for continuing to attack him with his weapons, and wonders that he does not seek new prey.

O Cupid, lodged in my heart but doing nothing
for me:

> quid me, qui miles numquam tua signa reliqui,
>   laedis, et in castris vulneror ipse meis?
> cur tua fax urit, <u>figit</u> tuus arcus amicos?
>   gloria pugnantes vincere maior erat.
> <u>venator</u> sequitur fugientia; capta relinquit   5
>   semper et inventis ulteriora petit.
> nos tua sentimus, populus tibi <u>deditus</u>, arma;
>   <u>pigra</u> reluctanti cessat in hoste manus.
> quid iuvat in nudis <u>hamata</u> <u>retundere</u> tela
>   ossibus? ossa mihi nuda relinquit amor.   10
> tot sine amore viri, tot sunt sine amore puellae
>   hinc tibi cum magna laude triumphus eat!
> Roma, nisi immensum vires <u>promosset</u> in orbem,
>   <u>stramineis</u> esset nunc quoque tecta <u>casis</u>.
> fessus in acceptos miles deducitur agros;   15
>   mittitur in <u>saltus</u> <u>carcere</u> liber equus;
> longaque <u>subductam</u> celant <u>navalia</u> pinum,
>   tutaque deposito poscitur ense <u>rudis</u>.
> me quoque, qui totiens <u>merui</u> sub amore puellae,
>   <u>defunctum</u> placide vivere tempus erat.   20

                        AMORES II

figo, -ere, fixi, fixum	I pierce
venator, -oris (m.)	hunter
deditus, -a, -um	surrendered
piger, -gra,-grum	lazy
hamatus, -a, -um	barbed
retundo, -ere, -tudi, -tusum	I blunt, hammer against
promosset	= *promovisset*
stramineus, -a, -um	made of straw
casa, -ae (f.)	hut
saltus, -us (m.)	glade, field
carcer, -eris (n.)	(*here*) starting block
subduco, -ere, -duxi, -ductum	I haul up on shore, beach

navalia, -um (n.pl.)	dockyard
rudis, -is (f.)	foil (*the wooden sword given to freed gladiators*)
mereo, -ere, -ui, -itum	(*here*) I serve as a soldier
defungor, -i, defunctus sum	I discharge (a duty)

(a) In lines 1–2 (*quid . . . meis*), what point do you think Ovid is making to Cupid? [2]

(b) Lines 1–4 (*quid . . . erat*): how do Ovid's choice of words and other stylistic features underline his feeling that he has been unjustly treated? Make **two** points and refer to the Latin. [4]

(c) In lines 5–6 (*venator . . . petit*), what comparison is Ovid drawing? Explain in your own words how it fits into Ovid's argument. [2+2]

(d) Lines 7–12 (*nos . . . eat*): how does Ovid, by his style and choice of detail, convey his indignation at Cupid's incessant assaults? Make **three** points and refer to the Latin. [6]

(e) Translate lines 11–20 (*tot . . . erat*) into good English. **Please write your translation on alternate lines.** [30]

(f) Write out and scan lines 19–20 (*me . . . erat*). [4]

Total [50]

Elegiac Passage 28 *Paris' love for Helen I*

Paris has fallen in love with Helen, wife of Menelaus, at whose home he is staying
as a guest. He describes how hard it is for him to restrain his emotions.

I turn my head away from you, but your very being
calls back my gaze at once.

quid faciam, dubito; dolor est meus illa videre,
    sed dolor a facie maior abesse tua.
qua licet et possum, luctor celare furorem,
    sed tamen apparet dissimulatus amor.
nec tibi verba damus; sentis mea vulnera, sentis;   5
    atque utinam soli sint ea nota tibi!
a, quotiens lacrimis venientibus ora reflexi,
    ne causam fletus quaereret ille mei.
a, quotiens aliquem narravi potus amorem,
    ad vultus referens singula verba tuos,   10
indiciumque mei ficto sub nomine feci;
    ille ego, si nescis, verus amator eram.
quin etiam, ut possem verbis petulantius uti,
    non semel ebrietas est simulata mihi.
prodita sunt, memini, tunica tua pectora laxa   15
    atque oculis aditum nuda dedere meis,
pectora vel puris nivibus vel lacte tuamve
    complexo matrem candidiora Iove.[1]
dum stupeo visis—nam pocula forte tenebam—
    tortilis a digitis excidit ansa meis.   20
oscula si natae dederas, ego protinus illa
    Hermiones tenero laetus ab ore tuli.

                              HEROIDES XVI

furor, -oris (m.)	passion
dissimulo, -are, -avi, -atum	I keep secret, cover up
ille	*refers to Menelaus*
potus, -a, -um	drunk
indicium, -ii (n.)	hint, indication
fictus, -a, -um	invented, pretend
quin	(*here*) what is more
petulans, -antis	bold, uninhibited

---

[1] Helen's mother Leda conceived Helen when Jupiter came to her in the form of a swan.

ebrietas, -atis (f.)	drunkenness
laxus, -a, -um	loose
aditus, -us (m.)	access
lac, lactis (n.)	milk
poculum, -i (n.)	cup
tortilis, -e	twisted
ansa, -ae (f.)	handle
Hermione, -es (Gk decl.) (f.)	Hermione (*Helen's daughter*)

(a) In lines 1–2 (*quid . . . tua*), what is Paris' problem? [2]

(b) Write out and scan lines 1–2 (*quid . . . tua*). [4]

(c) In lines 3–6 (*qua . . . tibi*), how does Ovid's language suggest Paris' vain struggle to conceal his true feelings? Make **three** points and refer to the Latin. [6]

(d) Look at lines 7–8 (*a, quotiens . . . mei*):

    (i) when did Paris turn his face away? [1]

    (ii) why did he do so? [2]

(e) Translate lines 9–18 (*a, quotiens . . . Iove*) into good English. **Please write your translation on alternate lines.** [30]

(f) In lines 19–20 (*dum . . . meis*), what was the effect of what he saw on Paris? Answer in detail. [3]

(g) Lines 21–22 (*oscula . . . tuli*): how did Paris use Hermione to soothe the agony of his love for Helen? [2]

Total [50]

Elegiac Passage 29 *Paris' love for Helen II*

Writing to her before the Trojan War, Paris tries to persuade Helen to leave her
husband, Menelaus, and return with him as his lover to Troy.

Even your foolish husband seems to want you to come
away with me – he's gone off to Crete and left us alone!

sola iaces viduo tam longa nocte <u>cubili</u>;
   in viduo iaceo solus et ipse toro.
te mihi meque tibi communia gaudia iungant;
   candidior medio nox erit illa die.
tunc ego iurabo <u>quaevis</u> tibi numina meque   5
   <u>adstringam</u> verbis in sacra vestra meis;
tunc ego, si non est fallax <u>fiducia</u> nostri,
   efficiam <u>praesens</u>, ut mea regna petas.
si <u>pudet</u> et metuis ne me videare secuta,
   ipse <u>reus</u> sine te criminis huius ero.   10
Troia classis adest armis instructa virisque;
   iam facient celeres remus et aura vias.
ibis <u>Dardanias</u> ingens regina per urbes,
   teque novam credet vulgus adesse deam,
<u>quaque</u> feres <u>gressus</u>, <u>adolebunt</u> <u>cinnama</u> flammae,   15
   caesaque sanguineam victima planget humum.
dona pater fratresque et cum genetrice sorores
   <u>Iliades</u>que omnes totaque Troia dabit.
ei mihi! pars a me vix dicitur ulla futuri.
   plura feres quam quae littera nostra refert.   20
nec tu rapta time, ne nos fera bella sequantur,
   concitet et vires Graecia magna suas.
tot prius abductis <u>ecqua</u> est repetita per arma?
   crede mihi, <u>vanos</u> res habet <u>ista</u> metus.

                       HEROIDES XVI

cubile, -is (n.)	bed
quivis, quaevis, quodvis	whatever … you want
adstringo, -ere, -strinxi, -strictum	I join to
fiducia, -ae (f.)	confidence
praesens, -entis	in person
pudet, -ere, puduit (impers.)	… is/are ashamed
reus, -i (m.)	defendant
Dardanius, -a, -um	Trojan

qua	where
gressus, -us (m.)	step, pace
adoleo, -ere, -ui	I burn (in sacrifice)
cinnama, -orum (n.pl.)	cinnamon branches
Iliades, -um (f.pl.)	women of Troy
ecqua . . .?	'is there a single girl who . . .?'
vanus, -a, -um	empty, groundless
iste, -a, -ud	(= *ille*) that, those

(a) In lines 1–6 (*sola . . . meis*), how does Ovid, by his choice and position of words, convey the shared love which Paris hopes for? Make **three** points and refer to the Latin. [6]

(b) Look at lines 7–8 (*tunc . . . petas*):

    (i) what does Paris hope he will achieve? [2]

    (ii) what is he relying on? [1]

    (iii) write out and scan these lines. [4]

(c) According to line 9 (*si . . . secuta*), why might Helen be unwilling to come? [2]

(d) *criminis* (line 10): to what does this refer? [1]

(e) Translate lines 11–20 (*Troia . . . refert*) into good English. **Please write your translation on alternate lines.** [30]

(f) The abduction of Helen by Paris did, of course, lead to war. How do you think Ovid conveys the irony of Paris' statements in lines 21–24 (*nec . . . metus*) by his choice and position of words? Make **two** points and refer to the Latin. [4]

Total [50]

Elegiac Passage 30 *The delights of dinner parties*

Ovid advises his male readers to make full use of the opportunities for love which dinner parties afford. He tells them that wine is a great help to them, but warns them to be a little careful of some of its effects.

I have told you how military triumphs can present opportunities for finding a girl. And now another idea:

dant etiam positis aditum convivia mensis:
    est aliquid praeter vina, quod inde petas.
saepe illic positi teneris adducta lacertis
    purpureus Bacchi cornua pressit Amor:
vinaque cum bibulas sparsere Cupidinis alas,   5
    permanet et capto stat gravis ille loco.
ille quidem pennas velociter excutit udas:
    sed tamen et spargi pectus amore nocet.
vina parant animos faciuntque caloribus aptos:
    cura fugit multo diluiturque mero.   10
tunc veniunt risus, tum pauper cornua sumit,
    tum dolor et curae rugaque frontis abit.
tunc aperit mentes aevo rarissima nostro
    simplicitas, artes excutiente deo.
illic saepe animos iuvenum rapuere puellae,   15
    et Venus in vinis ignis in igne fuit.
hic tu fallaci nimium ne crede lucernae:
    iudicio formae noxque merumque nocent.
luce deas caeloque Paris spectavit aperto,
    cum dixit Veneri 'vincis utramque, Venus.'   20
nocte latent mendae, vitioque ignoscitur omni,
    horaque formosam quamlibet illa facit.

                    ARS AMATORIA I

convivium, -ii (n.)	dinner party
positus, -a, -um	(*here*) lying, reclining
Bacchus, -i (m.)	Bacchus (*god of wine*)
premo, -ere, pressi, pressum	(*here*) I grasp, clasp hold of
bibulus, -a, -um	thirsty
calor, -oris (m.)	passion
diluo, -ere, -lui, -lutum	I wash away
risus, -us (m.)	laughter
ruga, -ae (f.)	crease, furrow

aevum, -i (n.)	age, era
lucerna, -ae (f.)	lamp
iudicium, -ii (n.)	judgment
Paris, -idis (m.)	Paris (*prince of Troy*)
utramque	*Paris had to judge which of three goddesses was the most beautiful.*
menda, -ae (f.)	fault
ignosco, -ere, -novi, -notum	I pardon, excuse
quilibet, quaelibet, quodlibet	any, anyone

(a) Explain what Ovid means in line 2 (*est aliquid praeter vina, quod inde petas*). [2]

(b) In lines 3–4 (*saepe . . . Amor*), what has Cupid often done to Bacchus? [1]

(c) In lines 5–8 (*vinaque . . . nocet*), what do you think Ovid is saying about the relationship between love and wine? Make **two** points and refer to the Latin. [4]

(d) From lines 9–10 (*vina . . . mero*), give **three** effects which Ovid says wine has. [3]

(e) In lines 9–12 (*vina . . . abit*), how does Ovid's language convey the soothing power of wine? Make **three** points and refer to the Latin in your answer. [6]

(f) Write out and scan lines 13–14 (*tunc . . . deo*). [4]

(g) Translate lines 13–22 (*tunc aperit . . . facit*) into good English. **Please write your translation on alternate lines.** [30]

Total [50]

Elegiac Passage 31 *The dangers of a sea voyage*

Ovid laments his girlfriend Corinna's decision to make a journey by sea and fears
the many potential dangers which await her.

It was the Argo which first taught men to sail
the dangerous paths of the sea.

o utinam, nequis remo freta longa moveret,
  Argo funestas pressa bibisset aquas!
ecce, fugit notumque torum sociosque Penates
  fallacesque vias ire Corinna parat.
quam tibi, me miserum, Zephyros Eurosque timebo   5
  et gelidum Borean egelidumque Notum!
non illic urbes, non tu mirabere silvas;
  una est iniusti caerula forma maris.
nec medius tenues conchas pictosque lapillos
  pontus habet; bibuli litoris illa mora est.   10
litora marmoreis pedibus signate, puellae;
  hactenus est tutum—cetera caeca via est.
et vobis alii ventorum proelia narrent;
  quas Scylla infestet, quasve Charybdis aquas;
et quibus emineant violenta Ceraunia saxis;   15
  quo lateant Syrtes magna minorque sinu.
haec alii referant ad vos; quod quisque loquetur,
  credite! credenti nulla procella nocet.
sero respicitur tellus, ubi fune soluto
  currit in immensum panda carina salum;   20
navita sollicitus cum ventos horret iniquos
  et prope tam letum, quam prope cernit aquam.

AMORES II

Argo, -us (Gk decl.) (f.)	the Argo (*Jason's ship*)
egelidus, -a, -um	warm
concha, -ae (f.)	sea-shell
lapillus, -i (m.)	pebble
bibulus, -a, -um	thirsty
signo, -are, -avi, -atum	I mark
hactenus	as far as this
caecus, -a, -um	blind
Scylla, -ae (f.)	Scylla (*a sea monster*)
Charybdis, -is (f.)	Charybdis (*a whirlpool*)

emineo, -ere, -ui	I reach up from
Ceraunia, -orum (n.pl.)	the Ceraunian mountains
Syrtes, -is (f.)	Syrtes (*a sandbank*)
sero	too late
funis, -is (m.)	mooring cable
immensum . . . salum	'expanse of the sea'
pandus, -a, -um	curved
sollicitus, -a, -um	anxious

(a) Translate lines 1–10 (*o utinam . . . mora est*) into good English.
   Please write your translation on alternate lines. [30]

(b) In lines 11–12 (*litora . . . est*), what does Ovid urge Corinna to do,
   and why? [2+1]

(c) Look at lines 13–16 (*et vobis . . . sinu*):

   (i) how, according to Ovid, should Corinna discover the mysteries
      of the sea? [1]

   (ii) what effect do you think this list of places is supposed to
      achieve? [2]

   (iii) how does Ovid, by the choice, position and rhythm of his words,
      make this effect especially powerful? Make **two** points and refer
      to the Latin in your answer. [4]

(d) In lines 17–18 (*haec . . . nocet*), what point is Ovid trying to make to
   Corinna? [2]

(e) Lines 19–22 (*sero . . . aquam*): how do Ovid's style and language
   emphasize the dangers of the sea in these lines? Make **two** points
   and refer to the Latin. [4]

(f) Write out and scan lines 21–22 (*navita . . . aquam*). [4]

Total [50]

Elegiac Passage 32 *Penelope pines for Ulysses*

Penelope, after many years of waiting for her husband Ulysses to return from the Trojan War, describes her constant fear and sadness.

The war finished so long ago that now there
are fields and farms where Troy once stood.

victor abes, nec scire mihi, quae causa morandi,
    aut in quo lateas <u>ferreus</u> orbe, licet.
quisquis ad haec vertit <u>peregrinam</u> litora puppem,
    ille mihi de te multa rogatus abit,
quamque tibi reddat, si te modo viderit usquam,   5
    traditur huic digitis <u>charta</u> notata meis.
utilius starent etiam nunc moenia Phoebi[1]—
    <u>irascor</u> votis, heu, <u>levis</u> ipsa meis!
scirem ubi pugnares, et tantum bella timerem,
    et mea cum multis iuncta querela foret.   10
quid timeam, ignoro—timeo tamen omnia <u>demens</u>,
    et patet in curas area lata meas.
quaecumque aequor habet, quaecumque pericula tellus,
    tam longae causas suspicor esse morae.
haec ego dum stulte metuo, quae vestra <u>libido</u> est,   15
    esse <u>peregrino</u> captus amore potes.
fallar, et hoc crimen tenues <u>vanescat</u> in auras,
    neve, revertendi liber, abesse velis!
me pater <u>Icarius</u> viduo discedere lecto
    cogit et immensas <u>increpat</u> usque moras.   20
<u>increpet</u> usque licet—tua sum, tua dicar <u>oportet</u>;
    <u>Penelope</u> coniunx semper <u>Ulixis</u> ero.

                                    HEROIDES I

ferreus, -a, -um	made of iron; hard-hearted
peregrinus, -a, -um	foreign
charta, -ae (f.)	sheet of paper
irascor, -i, iratus sum	I grow angry
levis, -e	(*here*) inconstant, fickle
demens, -entis	out of one's mind, mad
libido, -inis (f.)	lust, desire
vanesco, -ere, vanui	I vanish

---

[1] '*moenia Phoebi*' refers to Troy: Apollo had helped to build the walls of the city.

Icarius, -ii (m.)	Icarius (*Penelope's father*)
increpo, -are, -ui, -itum	I tell off, rebuke
oportet, -ere, -uit (impers.)	it is fitting, is right
Penelope, -es (Gk decl.) (f.)	Penelope (*wife of Ulysses*)
Ulixes, -is (m.)	Ulysses

(a) Translate lines 1–10 (*victor . . . foret*) into good English. **Please write your translation on alternate lines.** [30]

(b) In lines 11–12 (*quid . . . meas*), how does Penelope's language convey the strength of her fears? Make **two** points and refer to the Latin in your answer. [4]

(c) In lines 13–14 (*quaecumque . . . morae*), what **two** things does Penelope suspect to be responsible for Ulysses' absence? [2]

(d) Look at lines 15–16 (*haec . . . potes*):

   (i) what does Penelope fear here? [2]

   (ii) write out and scan these lines. [4]

(e) Lines 17–18 (*fallar . . . velis*): summarize in your own words what Penelope is praying for here. [2]

(f) In lines 19–20 (*me . . . moras*), what is the attitude of Penelope's father to Ulysses' long absence? [2]

(g) Look at lines 21–22 (*increpet . . . ero*): how does Ovid, by the style and content of his words, emphasize Penelope's determination to remain loyal to Ulysses? Make **two** points and refer to the Latin in your answer. [4]

Total [50]

Elegiac Passage 33　*Ovid resents the dawn*

Dawn arrives, and Ovid laments her coming, as she brings an end to pleasant rest and heralds the recommencement of daily toils.

The poem begins:

iam super Oceanum venit a seniore marito[1]
　flava pruinoso quae vehit axe diem.
nunc iuvat in teneris dominae iacuisse lacertis;
　si quando, lateri nunc bene iuncta meo est.
nunc etiam somni pingues et frigidus aer,　　　　　　5
　et liquidum tenui gutture cantat avis.
quo properas ingrata viris, ingrata puellis?
　roscida purpurea supprime lora manu.
ante tuos ortus melius sua sidera servat
　navita nec media nescius errat aqua;　　　　　　10
te surgit quamvis lassus veniente viator,
　et miles saevas aptat ad arma manus;
prima bidente vides oneratos arva colentes,
　prima vocas tardos sub iuga panda boves.
tu pueros somno fraudas tradisque magistris,　　　　15
　ut subeant tenerae verbera saeva manus;
nec tu consulto, nec tu iucunda diserto;
　cogitur ad lites surgere uterque novas.
tu, cum feminei possint cessare labores,
　lanificam revocas ad sua pensa manum.　　　　　　20
　　　　　　　　　　　　　　　　AMORES I

Oceanus, -i (m.)	Oceanus (*the river which flowed around the world*)
senior, -oris	(*here*) too old
pruinosus, -a, -um	frosty
pinguis, -e	deep, heavy
roscidus, -a, -um	dripping with dew, dewy
lora, -orum (n.pl.)	reins
bidens, -entis (m.)	a hoe with two teeth
oneratus, -a, -um	burdened
colentes	'those who plough'
pandus, -a, -um	bent, curved

[1]　Dawn's husband was Tithonus, a Trojan prince. When asking for his immortality, she omitted to ask for eternal youth, and so he lived forever, getting older and older.

fraudo, -are, -avi, -atum	I cheat, trick
verber, -eris (n.)	beating, blow
consultus, -i (m.)	lawyer
disertus, -i (m.)	advocate
lis, litis (f.)	legal case
lanificus, -a, -um	wool-making
pensum, -i (n.)	work

(a) Lines 1–2 (*iam . . . diem*): how is Dawn's arrival described?   [2]

(b) In lines 3–4 (*nunc . . . est*), for what **two** reasons is Ovid unwilling to
leave his bed?   [2]

(c) Translate lines 5–14 (*nunc . . . boves*) into good English. **Please write
your translation on alternate lines.**   [30]

(d) Write out and scan lines 15–16 (*tu . . . manus*).   [4]

(e) In lines 15–16 (*tu . . . manus*), what will the boys suffer, and at whose
hands?   [2]

(f) Lines 17–18 (*nec . . . novas*): how is Dawn received by lawyers, and
why?   [2]

(g) What point do you think Ovid is trying to make by the accumulation of
examples in lines 9–20?   [2]

(h) Look at lines 15–20 (*tu . . . manum*): how does Ovid, through his choice
and arrangement of words, emphasize how unwelcome Dawn's arrival is?
Make **three** points and refer closely to the Latin in your answer.   [6]

Total [50]

Elegiac Passage 34 *Aeneas and Dido*

Dido, queen of Carthage, welcomed the Trojan prince Aeneas to her land, and the
two soon fell in love. Now, as Aeneas prepares to depart to find his promised land
(Italy), Dido asks if he really intends to break his word.

I know you will not be moved by my words, but
still I write to you.

certus es ire tamen miseramque relinquere Didon
    atque idem venti vela fidemque ferent?
certus es, Aenea, cum foedere solvere naves
    quaeque ubi sint nescis, Itala regna sequi?
nec nova Karthago, nec te crescentia tangunt   5
    moenia nec sceptro tradita summa tuo?
facta fugis, facienda petis; quaerenda per orbem
    altera, quaesita est altera terra tibi.
ut terram invenias, quis eam tibi tradet habendam?
    quis sua non notis arva tenenda dabit?   10
alter habendus amor tibi restat et altera Dido
    quamque iterum fallas, altera danda fides.
quando erit, ut condas instar Karthaginis urbem
    et videas populos altus ab arce tuos?
omnia ut eveniant, nec di tua vota morentur,   15
    unde tibi, quae te sic amet, uxor erit?
Aeneas oculis vigilantis semper inhaeret;
    Aenean animo noxque diesque refert.
ille quidem male gratus et ad mea munera surdus
    et quo, si non sim stulta, carere velim.   20
non tamen Aenean, quamvis male cogitat, odi,
    sed queror infidum questaque peius amo.

                        HEROIDES VII

Dido (Gk acc. *Didon*) (f.)	Dido (*queen of Carthage*)
Aeneas (Gk voc. *Aenea*; acc. *-ean*) (m.)	Aeneas (*a Trojan prince*)
foedus, -eris (n.)	treaty, promise
Italus, -a, -um	Italian
Karthago, -inis (f.)	Carthage
summa, -ae (f.)	highest power
ut	(*here*) even if
resto, -stare, -stiti	I remain
fallo, -ere, fefelli, falsum	(*here*) I break, prove false

instar (+ gen.)	like
vigilo, -are, -avi, -atum	I am awake
inhaereo, -ere, -haesi, -haesum	I stick to, cling to

(a) In lines 1–4 (*certus . . . sequi*), how does Ovid convey Dido's emotion at Aeneas' decision to leave? Make **two** points and refer to the Latin.   [4]

(b) In line 4 (*quaeque . . . sequi*), what does Dido say to highlight the difficulty of Aeneas' mission?   [1]

(c) In lines 5–6 (*nec . . . tuo*), what **three** enticements does Dido give to Aeneas to stay?   [3]

(d) In lines 7–8 (*facta . . . tibi*), how does Dido's language suggest the folly of Aeneas' decision to depart? Make **two** points and refer to the Latin.   [4]

(e) In lines 9–10 (*ut . . . dabit*), what objections does Dido make to Aeneas' plans?   [2]

(f) Write out and scan lines 9–10 (*ut . . . dabit*).   [4]

(g) What does Dido say in lines 11–12 (*alter . . . fides*) which implies bitterness at her treatment by Aeneas?   [2]

(h) Translate lines 13–22 (*quando . . . amo*) into good English. **Please write your translation on alternate lines.**   [30]

Total [50]

Elegiac Passage 35 *Love objects to Ovid's work*

Ovid begins the *Cures for Love* by telling how Cupid resented such a work. The poet tells Cupid not to fight him – he remains Love's devoted servant.

The poem begins:

> legerat huius Amor titulum nomenque libelli:
>   'bella mihi, video, bella parantur' ait.
> parce tuum vatem sceleris damnare, Cupido,
>   tradita qui toties te duce signa tuli.
> non ego Tydides, a quo tua saucia mater   5
>   in liquidum rediit aethera Martis equis.[1]
> saepe tepent alii iuvenes: ego semper amavi,
>   et si, quid faciam, nunc quoque, quaeris, amo.
> nec te, blande puer, nec nostras prodimus artes,
>   nec nova praeteritum Musa retexit opus.   10
> siquis amat quod amare iuvat, feliciter ardens
>   gaudeat, et vento naviget ille suo.
> at siquis male fert indignae regna puellae,
>   ne pereat, nostrae sentiat artis opem.
> cur aliquis rigido fodit sua pectora ferro?   15
>   invidiam caedis, pacis amator, habes.
> et puer es, nec te quicquam nisi ludere oportet:
>   lude; decent annos mollia regna tuos.
> vitricus et gladiis et acuta dimicet hasta,
>   et victor multa caede cruentus eat: 20
> tu cole maternas, tuto quibus utimur, artes,
>   et quarum vitio nulla fit orba parens.
>
>   REMEDIA AMORIS

titulum, -i (n.)	title
libellus, -i (m.)	little book
parce (+ infin.)	don't
toties	so often
Tydides, -is (m.)	son of Tydeus (= *Diomedes*)
mater	*Cupid's mother is Venus*
praeteritus, -a, -um	previous
retego, -ere, -texi, -tectum	I reveal, uncover
invidia, -ae (f.)	ill-will, hatred

---

[1]   In Book V of Homer's *Iliad*, the Greek hero Diomedes wounds Aphrodite (= Venus) on the battlefield, and she is forced to beg Ares (= Mars) for his horses to escape.

oportet, -ere, -uit (impers.)	it is fitting
deceo, -ere, -ui	I am appropriate for
mollis, -e	gentle
vitricus, -i (m.)	step-father (*i.e.* Mars)

(a) Look at lines 1–2 (*legerat . . . ait*):

    (i) how does Cupid interpret Ovid's decision to write this new work? [1]

    (ii) why do you think he interprets it in this way? [2]

    (iii) how does his language convey a sense of outrage? [2]

(b) What imagery is Ovid using in line 4 (*tradita . . . tuli*)? Pick out and translate **two** Latin words which generate this imagery. [1+2]

(c) In lines 5–6 (*non . . . equis*), what point do you think Ovid is making about himself by this reference to mythology? [2]

(d) In lines 7–12 (*saepe . . . suo*), how does Ovid's language emphasize his unshakable commitment to love? Make **three** points and refer to the Latin. [6]

(e) Translate lines 13–22 (*at . . . parens*) into good English. **Please write your translation on alternate lines.** [30]

(f) Write out and scan lines 21–22 (*tu . . . parens*). [4]

Total [50]

Elegiac Passage 36 *Ceres and Persephone*

While Ceres (goddess of the harvest) is at a feast of the mother-gods, her daughter Persephone is picking flowers in the fields of Sicily. But her uncle Pluto, god of the Underworld, captivated by her beauty, carries Persephone off to his realm.

The river nymph Arethusa had called all the mother-gods
to a banquet, and Ceres attended with many others.

filia, consuetis ut erat <u>comitata</u> puellis,
    errabat nudo per sua prata pede.
valle sub umbrosa locus est <u>aspergine</u> multa
    uvidus ex alto desilientis aquae.
tot fuerant illic, quot habet natura, colores,   5
    floribus et variis picta nitebat humus.
quam simul aspexit, 'comites, accedite' dixit
    'et mecum plenos flore referte sinus.'
plurima lecta rosa est, sunt et sine nomine flores:
    ipsa <u>crocos</u> tenues <u>lilia</u>que alba legit.   10
<u>carpendi</u> studio paulatim longius ibat,
    et dominam casu nulla secuta comes.
hanc videt et visam <u>patruus</u> velociter aufert
    regnaque caeruleis in sua portat equis.
illa quidem clamabat 'io, carissima mater,   15
    auferor!', ipsa suos <u>absciderat</u>que sinus:
at chorus <u>aequalis</u>, <u>cumulatae</u> flore <u>ministrae</u>
    '<u>Persephone</u>', clamant 'ad tua dona veni!'
ut clamata silet, montes <u>ululatibus</u> implent,
    et feriunt maesta pectora nuda manu.   20
attonita est <u>plangore</u> <u>Ceres</u> (modo venerat <u>Hennam</u>)
    nec mora, 'me miseram! filia' dixit 'ubi es?'
                            FASTI IV

comitatus, -a, -um	accompanied
aspergo, -inis (f.)	spray
crocus, -i (m.)	crocus
lilium, -i (n.)	lily
carpo, -ere, -psi, -ptum	I pluck
patruus, -ui (m.)	uncle (*i.e. Pluto*)
io!	(*here*) quick!, help!
abscindo, -ere, -scidi, -scissum	I tear from
aequalis, -e	of equal age, of peers

cumulo, -are, -avi, -atum	I heap up
ministra, -ae (f.)	attendant, servant
Persephone, -es (Gk decl.) (f.)	Persephone
ululatus, -us (m.)	wailing
plangor, -oris (m.)	lamentation
Ceres, -eris (f.)	Ceres
Henna, -ae (f.)	Enna (*a town in Sicily*)

(a) Translate lines 1–10 (*filia . . . legit*) into good English. **Please write your translation on alternate lines.** [30]

(b) Look at lines 11–12 (*carpendi . . . comes*):

    (i)   what does Persephone do? [1]

    (ii)   what leads her to do this? [1]

    (iii) why is this potentially dangerous for her? [2]

(c) In lines 13–16 (*hanc . . . sinus*), how do Ovid's choice and position of words dramatize the abduction of Persephone? Make **two** points and refer to the Latin. [4]

(d) In lines 17–18 (*at . . . veni*), what do the girls call Persephone back to? To what are they referring? [2]

(e) Lines 19–20 (*ut . . . manu*): in what **two** ways do the girls show their distress? [2]

(f) Write out and scan lines 19–20 (*ut . . . manu*). [4]

(g) Lines 19–22 (*ut . . . es*): how do the choice, position and rhythm of Ovid's words help to describe the grief caused by Persephone's disappearance? Make **two** points and refer to the Latin. [4]

Total [50]

Elegiac Passage 37 *Cupid's triumph*

Ovid admits that Cupid is the master of all things. He tells him to celebrate a triumph like a victorious general, parading all he has conquered.

I confess, Cupid, I am your prisoner and I submit totally to you.
There's no need to fight, I'm unarmed against you!

necte comam myrto, maternas iunge columbas;	
qui deceat, currum vitricus ipse dabit,	
inque dato curru, populo clamante 'triumphum',	
stabis et adiunctas arte movebis aves.	
ducentur capti iuvenes captaeque puellae;	5
haec tibi magnificus pompa triumphus erit.	
ipse ego, praeda recens, factum modo vulnus habebo	
et nova captiva vincula mente feram.	
omnia te metuent; ad te sua bracchia tendens	
vulgus 'io' magna voce 'triumphe!' canet.	10
blanditiae comites tibi erunt Errorque Furorque,	
adsidue partes turba secuta tuas.	
his tu militibus superas hominesque deosque;	
haec tibi si demas commoda, nudus eris.	
laeta triumphanti de summo mater Olympo	15
plaudet et adpositas sparget in ora rosas.	
tu pennas gemma, gemma variante capillos	
ibis in auratis aureus ipse rotis.	
tunc quoque non paucos, si te bene novimus, ures;	
tunc quoque praeteriens vulnera multa dabis.	20
ergo cum possim sacri pars esse triumphi,	
parce tuas in me perdere, victor, opes!	

AMORES I

necto, -ere, nexui, nexum	I tie, bind
myrtus, -i (f.)	myrtle
vitricus, -i (m.)	step-father (*i.e. Mars*)
pompa, -ae (f.)	procession
io!	hooray!
blanditia, -ae (f.)	flattery
Error, -oris (m.)	Mistake (*personified*)
Furor, -oris (m.)	Wild Passion (*personified*)
adsidue	continually
demo, -ere, dempsi, demptum	I take away

commodum, -i (n.)	advantage, help
triumpho, -are, -avi, -atum	I celebrate a triumph
Olympus, -i (m.)	Mount Olympus (*home of the gods*)
plaudo, -ere, -si, -sum	I applaud
auratus, -a, -um	covered in gold
rota, -ae (f.)	(*here*) chariot
parce (+ infin.)	don't

(a) Translate lines 1–10 (*necte . . . canet*) into good English. **Please write your translation on alternate lines.** [30]

(b) Look at lines 11–14 (*blanditiae . . . eris*):

    (i) write down **two** details mentioned by Ovid in these lines which show how closely linked *Error* and *Furor* are to Cupid. [2]

    (ii) why do you think Ovid characterizes *Error* and *Furor* in this way? [2]

    (iii) write out and scan lines 13–14 (*his . . . eris*). [4]

(c) In lines 15–16 (*laeta . . . rosas*), what will Cupid's mother do? [2]

(d) In lines 17–18 (*tu . . . rotis*), how does Ovid's language evoke the splendour of Cupid's triumph? Make **two** points and refer to the Latin. [4]

(e) Lines 19–20 (*tunc . . . dabis*):

    (i) what else does Ovid believe Cupid will do? [2]

    (ii) pick out and translate the phrase which tells us that Ovid has long experience of Cupid's methods. [2]

(f) In lines 21–22 (*ergo . . . opes*), what does Ovid ask for and why does he feel he deserves it? [1+1]

Total [50]

Elegiac Passage 38 *Forbidden fruits*

Ovid warns a protective husband not to try to guard his wife from others with
look-outs and locks: this, he says, only excites the desires of a lover.

The poem begins:

dure vir, imposito tenerae custode puellae
    <u>nil agis</u>; ingenio est quaeque <u>tuenda</u> suo.
<u>ut</u> iam servaris bene corpus, adultera mens est;
    nec custodiri, ne velit, ulla potest.
nec corpus servare potes, <u>licet</u> omnia claudas;   5
    omnibus exclusis intus adulter erit.
cui <u>peccare</u> licet, <u>peccat</u> minus; ipsa potestas
    semina <u>nequitiae</u> <u>languidiora</u> facit.
desine, crede mihi, vitia <u>inritare</u> vetando;
    <u>obsequio</u> vinces aptius illa tuo.   10
vidi ego nuper equum contra sua vincla <u>tenacem</u>
    ore reluctanti fulminis ire <u>modo</u>;
constitit <u>ut primum</u> concessas sensit habenas
    frenaque in effusa <u>laxa</u> iacere <u>iuba</u>!
nitimur in vetitum semper cupimusque negata;   15
    sic <u>interdictis</u> <u>imminet</u> aeger aquis.
centum fronte oculos, centum cervice gerebat
    <u>Argus</u>—et hos unus saepe fefellit Amor;
in thalamum <u>Danae</u> ferro saxoque perennem
    quae fuerat virgo tradita, mater erat;   20
<u>Penelope</u> mansit, quamvis custode carebat,
    inter tot iuvenes <u>intemerata</u> <u>procos</u>.
                  AMORES III

nil agis	'you achieve nothing'
tueor, -eri, tutus sum	I protect
ut	(*here*) although
licet	(*here*) even though
pecco, -are, -avi, -atum	I sin
nequitia, -ae (f.)	wickedness
languidus, -a, -um	weak
inrito, -are, -avi, -atum	I excite, stir up
obsequium, -ii (n.)	indulgence
tenax, -acis	obstinate, stubborn
modo (+ gen.)	like ..., in the manner of ...

ut primum	as soon as
laxus, -a, -um	loose, slack
iuba, -ae (f.)	horse's mane
interdico, -ere, -dixi, -dictum	I forbid
immineo, -ere, -ui	(*here*) I long for
Argus, -i (m.)	Argus[1]
Danae, -aes (Gk decl.) (f.)	Danae[2]
Penelope, -es (Gk decl.) (f.)	Penelope (*Ulysses' wife*)
intemeratus, -a, -um	untouched, pure
procus, -i (m.)	suitor

(a) Translate lines 1–10 (*dure . . . tuo*) into good English. **Please write your translation on alternate lines.** [30]

(b) Look at lines 11–14 (*vidi . . . iuba*):

   (i) explain in your own words the point Ovid is trying to illustrate in these lines. [3]

   (ii) how does Ovid's language make his allegory particularly powerful and effective? Make **two** points and refer to the Latin. [4]

(c) Write out and scan lines 13–14 (*constitit . . . iuba*). [4]

(d) *nitimur . . . aquis* (lines 15–16): to what else does Ovid compare a lover's desire for the forbidden? [1]

(e) In lines 17–18 (*centum . . . Amor*), what made Argus such a formidable guard? [2]

(f) *centum . . . procos* (lines 17–22): how does Ovid use language to make his examples from myth effective for his argument? Make **three** points and refer to the Latin. [6]

Total [50]

---

[1]   Argus was a giant whom Juno appointed to guard Io from Jupiter's advances. However, Jupiter ordered Mercury, or in Ovid's version Cupid, to send Argus to sleep and kill him.

[2]   Danae's father Acrisius had heard a prophecy that his daughter's son would kill him. He therefore locked her away in a secure chamber. But Jupiter, in love with Danae, came to her through the keyhole of the room as a shower of gold.

Elegiac Passage 39 *Hypsipyle awaits news of Jason*

When Jason stopped on the island of Lemnos, he impregnated the island's queen Hypsipyle and promised to love her forever. But the hero faithlessly abandoned Hypsipyle, leaving her desperate for news.

How I wish it was letters from you, rather than rumours,
which kept me informed of your progress!

quid queror officium lenti cessasse mariti?
  obsequium, maneo si tua, grande tuli.
barbara narratur venisse venefica tecum
  in mihi promissi parte recepta tori.
credula res amor est. utinam temeraria dicar   5
  criminibus falsis insimulasse virum!
nuper ab Haemoniis hospes mihi Thessalus oris
  venerat et tactum vix bene limen erat,
'Aesonides,' dixi, 'quid agit meus?' ille pudore
  haesit in opposita lumina fixus humo.   10
protinus exsilui tunicisque a pectore ruptis
  'vivit? an,' exclamo, 'me quoque fata vocant?'
'vivit,' ait timidus; timidum iurare coegi.
  vix mihi teste deo credita vita tua est.
utque animus rediit, tua facta requirere coepi: 15
  narrat aeripedes Martis arasse boves,
vipereos dentes in humum pro semine iactos
  et subito natos arma tulisse viros.
devictus serpens. iterum, si vivat Iason,
  quaerimus; alternant spesque timorque fidem.   20
singula dum narrat, studio cursuque loquendi
  detegit ingenio vulnera nostra suo.
heu, ubi pacta fides? ubi conubialia iura
  faxque sub arsuros dignior ire rogos?

                                        HEROIDES VI

obsequium, -ii (n.)	indulgence, treat
venefica, -ae (f.)	poisoner, sorceress
credulus, -a, -um	quick to believe, credulous
insimulo, -are, -avi, -atum	I accuse
Haemonius, -a, -um	of Thessaly (*a region of Greece*)
Thessalus, -a, -um	Thessalian (*from Thessaly*)
Aesonides, -is (m.)	son of Aeson (= *Jason*)

haereo, -ere, haesi, haesum	I stick, fix
opposita . . . humo	'the ground in front of him'
testis, -is (m.)	witness
requiro, -ere, -sivi, -situm	I ask about, inquire about
aeripes, -edis	with hooves of bronze
aro, -are, -avi, -atum	I plough
vipereus, -a, -um	of a snake
alterno, -are, -avi, -atum	I bring in turns
cursus, -us (m.)	(*here*) speed
detego, -ere, -texi, -tectum	I uncover
ingenium, -ii (n.)	skill (*i.e. at story-telling*)
conubialis, -e	of marriage

(a) Translate lines 1–10 (*quid . . . humo*) into good English. **Please write your translation on alternate lines.** [30]

(b) Look at lines 11–13 (*protinus . . . coegi*):

   (i) write out and scan lines 11–12 (*protinus . . . vocant*). [4]

   (ii) how do the language and rhythm of these lines form a vivid evocation of Hypsipyle's mental and physical turmoil? Make **two** points and refer to the Latin. [4]

(c) What do you think Hypsipyle means by her comment in line 14 (*vix . . . est*)? [2]

(d) Lines 16–18 (*narrat . . . viros*): what, in detail, are the **three** events which the Thessalian reports? [4]

(e) In lines 19–24 (*iterum . . . rogos*), how does Ovid's language evoke Hypsipyle's surging emotions? Make **three** points and refer closely to the Latin in your answer. [6]

Total [50]

Elegiac Passage 40 *The conception of Mars*

Flora, goddess of flowers, tells how she brought about the birth of Mars by
impregnating Juno with a magic flower. But shhh! don't tell Jupiter – he still
thinks he is the father.

Juno was upset that Jupiter had given birth to Athene
by himself, without a mother, without her.

ibat ut Oceano quereretur facta mariti;
    restitit ad nostras fessa labore fores.
quam simul aspexi, 'quid te, Saturnia', dixi
    'attulit?' exponit, quem petat illa locum,
addidit et causam. verbis solabar amicis.   5
    'non' inquit 'verbis cura levanda mea est.
si pater est factus neglecto coniugis usu
    Iuppiter, et solus nomen utrumque tenet,
cur ego desperem fieri sine coniuge mater,
    et parere intacto, dummodo casta, viro?   10
omnia temptabo latis medicamina terris,
    et freta Tartareos excutiamque sinus.'
ter volui promittere opem, ter lingua retenta est:
    ira Iovis magni causa timoris erat.
'fer, precor, auxilium' dixit, 'celabitur auctor',   15
    et Stygiae numen testificatur aquae.
'quod petis, Oleniis' inquam 'mihi missus ab arvis
    flos dabit: est hortis unicus ille meis.
qui dabat, "hoc" dixit "sterilem quoque tange iuvencam,
    mater erit": tetigi, nec mora, mater erat.'   20
protinus haerentem decerpsi pollice florem;
    tangitur, et tacto concipit illa sinu.

                                     FASTI V

Oceanus, -i (m.)	Oceanus (*god of the great river encircling the world*)
Saturnia, -ae (f.)	daughter of Saturn (= *Juno*)
expono, -ere, -posui, -positum	I explain
solor, -ari, -atus sum	I console
levo, -are, -avi, -atum	I alleviate, lessen
despero, -are, -avi, -atum	I despair, lose hope
intactus, -a, -um	untouched
Tartareus, -a, -um	of the Underworld

excutio, -ere, -cussi, -cussum	(*here*) I search
Stygius, -a, -um	of the Styx (*river of the Underworld*)
testificor, -ari, -atus sum	I call as a witness
Olenius, -a, -um	Aetolian (*region in Greece*)
unicus, -a, -um	unique, only . . . of its kind
sterilis, -e	infertile
iuvenca, -ae (f.)	heifer, young cow
haereo, -ere, haesi, haesum	I cling, stick
decerpo, -ere, -cerpsi, -cerptum	I pluck
pollex, -icis (m.)	thumb

(a) Translate lines 1–10 (*ibat . . . viro*) into good English. **Please write your translation on alternate lines.** [30]

(b) In lines 11–12 (*omnia . . . sinus*), how does Juno make clear her determination to find what she wants? Make **two** points. [2]

(c) Look at lines 13–14 (*ter . . . erat*):

   (i) how does Flora's language convey her eagerness to help? Make **one** point. [2]

   (ii) why does she not offer help? [2]

(d) Look at lines 15–16 (*fer . . . aquae*):

   (i) what promise does Juno make should Flora help her? [1]

   (ii) how does she make her promise binding? [2]

(e) In lines 17–18 (*quod . . . meis*), how does Flora say she came by this special flower? [1]

(f) In lines 17–20 (*quod . . . erat*), how do Flora's choice and position of words make clear the great powers of the flower? Make **two** points and refer to the Latin. [4]

(g) In lines 21–22 (*protinus . . . sinu*), how does Flora emphasize the flower's immediate impact? Make **one** point. [2]

(h) Write out and scan lines 21–22 (*protinus . . . sinu*). [4]

Total [50]

Ovid's Hexameter Poetry

Passages 1–20
Shorter translation passages

Passages 21–40
Full translation and comprehension passages

Hexameter Passage 1 *Cadmus and the dragon's teeth I*

Cadmus is ordered by Athene to sow the teeth of a giant serpent he has just killed
in the ground. When he does so, a terrible crop grows up.

With his spear Cadmus pinned the serpent to a tree, which
bent under its weight as it thrashed in its death throes.

dum <u>spatium</u> victor victi <u>considerat</u> hostis,
vox subito audita est; neque erat cognoscere <u>promptum</u>,
unde, sed audita est: 'quid, <u>Agenore nate</u>, <u>peremptum</u>
serpentem spectas? et tu spectabere serpens.'
ille diu pavidus pariter cum mente colorem   5
perdiderat, gelidoque comae terrore <u>rigebant</u>:
ecce viri <u>fautrix</u> superas delapsa per auras
Pallas adest motaeque iubet supponere terrae
vipereos dentes, populi <u>incrementa</u> futuri.
paret et, ut presso <u>sulcum</u> <u>patefecit</u> aratro,   10
spargit humi iussos, mortalia <u>semina</u>, dentes.
inde (<u>fide maius</u>) <u>glaebae</u> coepere moveri:
mox umeri pectusque <u>onerata</u>que bracchia telis
exsistunt, crescitque seges <u>clipeata</u> virorum.
                              METAMORPHOSES III

spatium, -ii (n.)	(*here*) size
considero, -are, -avi, -atum	I consider
promptus, -a, -um	(*here*) easy
Agenore natus, -i (m.)	son of Agenor (= *Cadmus*)
perimo, -ere, -emi, -emptum	I kill
rigeo, -ere	I stand on end
fautrix, -icis (f.)	supporter (*here, Athene*)
incrementum, -i (n.)	seed
sulcus, -i (m.)	furrow, ditch
patefacio, -ere, -feci, -factum	I make open
semen, -inis (n.)	seed
fide maius	beyond belief
glaeba, -ae (f.)	sod of earth
oneratus, -a, -um	burdened
clipeatus, -a, -um	carrying shields

DISCENDUM *-ere in the passive*

The shortened ending *-ere* can be used in verse as an alternative for the *-eris*
of the second person singular passive (present or future). So look at line 4:
spectabere = *spectaberis* ('you will be seen/watched'). Of course, be careful
not to confuse these with infinitives, which they deceptively resemble.

Hexameter Passage 2 *Cadmus and the dragon's teeth II*

(*Continued from the previous passage.*) Cadmus watches as the armed men immediately burst into a fight with one another, until only five remain alive.

The men arose like figures embroidered on a curtain: as it is pulled up, the men gradually appear.

territus hoste novo Cadmus capere arma parabat:
'ne cape!' de populo, quem terra creaverat, unus
exclamat 'nec te civilibus <u>insere</u> bellis!'
atque ita <u>terrigenis</u> rigido de fratribus unum
<u>comminus</u> ense ferit, <u>iaculo</u> cadit <u>eminus</u> ipse;   5
hunc quoque qui leto dederat, non longius illo
vivit et exspirat <u>modo</u> quas acceperat auras,
exemploque pari furit omnis turba, suoque
Marte cadunt <u>subiti</u> per <u>mutua</u> vulnera fratres.
iamque brevis vitae spatium <u>sortita</u> <u>iuventus</u>   10
sanguineam tepido <u>plangebat</u> pectore <u>matrem</u>,
quinque <u>superstitibus</u>, quorum fuit unus <u>Echion</u>.
is sua iecit humo monitu <u>Tritonidis</u> arma
fraternaeque fidem pacis petiitque deditque.

METAMORPHOSES III

insero, -ere, -ui, -sertum	I place (*acc.*) in the midst of (*abl.*)
terrigenus, -a, -um	born from the earth
comminus	at close quarters
iaculo . . . eminus	by a spear thrown from a distance
modo	only recently
subitus, -a, -um	short-lived
mutuus, -a, -um	mutual, reciprocal
sortior, -iri, -itus sum	I obtain by lot
iuventus, -utis (f.)	youth
plango, -ere, -nxi, -nctum	I pound on
matrem	*here refers to Mother Earth*
superstes, -stitis	surviving
Echion, -onis (m.)	Echion
Tritonis, -idis (f.)	Athene (*goddess of Lake Tritonis*)

DISCENDUM *Using glossed vocabulary*

As you will know, the same parts of glossed words are always given in the same order. For nouns, for example, that is: nom. sing., gen. sing., gender. Be sure to use all of this information, which can be reassuring when encountering new words; here, for example, it tells you that *Echion* must be nominative, while *Tritonidis* is genitive.

Hexameter Passage 3 *Lyncus becomes a lynx*

Ceres has sent the Athenian Triptolemus to spread her seeds over the land. When Lyncus of Scythia tries to kill Triptolemus, the goddess transforms him.

Ceres handed over her flying chariot to the young Triptolemus and told him to scatter her seed on both virgin and fallow soil.

iam super Europen sublimis et Asida terram
vectus erat iuvenis: Scythicas advertitur oras.
rex ibi Lyncus erat; regis subit ille Penates.
qua veniat, causamque viae nomenque rogatus
et patriam, 'patria est clarae mihi' dixit 'Athenae;   5
Triptolemus nomen; veni nec puppe per undas,
nec pede per terras: patuit mihi pervius aether.
dona fero Cereris, latos quae sparsa per agros
frugiferas messes alimentaque mitia reddant.'
barbarus invidit tantique ut muneris auctor   10
ipse sit, hospitio recipit somnoque gravatum
adgreditur ferro: conantem figere pectus
lynca Ceres fecit rursusque per aera iussit
Mopsopium iuvenem sacros agitare iugales.
                    METAMORPHOSES V

Europen/Asida	Greek accusatives
Scythicus, -a, -um	Scythian (*a tribe from Ukraine*)
Penates, -ium (m.pl.)	(*here*) home
qua	(*here*) how
pervius, -a, -um	navigable, traversable
Ceres, -eris (f.)	Ceres (*goddess of the harvest*)
frugifer, -era, -erum	fruit-bearing, fruitful
messis, -is (f.)	harvest
alimentum, -i (n.)	nourishment
gravo, -are, -avi, -atum	I weigh down
figo, -ere, fixi, fixum	I pierce
lynx, lyncis (Gk acc. *-a*) (c.)	lynx
Mopsopius, -a, -um	Athenian
iugales, -ium (m.pl.)	team of horses

DISCENDUM *Conjunctions out of place*

Look out for conjunctions (*et, ut, cum*, etc.) out of position. Take line 10: for *tantique ut* you may sensibly be thinking along the lines of 'and so great that ...', but in fact this will not get you anywhere. The *ut* is postponed from the beginning of the sentence, where it belongs in terms of sense. Your translation should be, 'in order that ... of so great a gift'. Beware: these out-of-place conjunctions are common and tricky.

Hexameter Passage 4 *Ceyx's departure*

Alcyone's husband Ceyx is departing on a sea voyage. But Alcyone, extremely worried for her husband's safety, is terrified as she watches him leave.

Ceyx ordered his ship to be launched and prepared for the journey:

horruit <u>Alcyone</u> lacrimasque emisit <u>obortas</u>
amplexusque dedit tristique miserrima tandem
ore 'vale' dixit collapsaque corpore toto est;
<u>ast</u> iuvenes quaerente moras <u>Ceyce</u> reducunt
ordinibus geminis ad fortia pectora <u>remos</u>   5
aequalique <u>ictu</u> <u>scindunt</u> freta: sustulit illa
<u>umentes</u> oculos stantemque in puppe recurva
concussaque manu dantem sibi signa maritum
prima videt redditque <u>notas</u>; ubi terra recessit
longius, atque oculi nequeunt cognoscere vultus,   10
dum licet, insequitur fugientem lumine <u>pinum</u>;
haec quoque ut haud poterat spatio submota videri,
vela tamen spectat summo <u>fluitantia</u> <u>malo</u>;
ut nec vela videt, <u>vacuum</u> petit anxia lectum
seque toro ponit.   15

METAMORPHOSES XI

Alcyone, -es (Gk decl.) (f.)	Alcyone
oborior, -iri, -ortus sum	I well up (*of tears*)
ast	but
Ceyx, Ceycis (m.)	Ceyx
remus, -i (m.)	oar
ictus, -us (m.)	blow, stroke
scindo, -ere, scidi, scissum	I cut
umeo, -ere	I am wet, moist
nota, -ae (f.)	sign, token
pinus, -us (f.)	(*here*) ship
fluito, -are, -avi	I flutter
malus, -i (m.)	mast
vacuus, -a, -um	empty

DISCENDUM *Translating 'ut'*

The use of *ut* in line 12 here is a good reminder of how tricky this word can be in verse. First remember that with the indicative, it does not mean 'in order to', etc., but simply 'as' or 'when'. Second, note that, like other conjunctions, it can be delayed from the beginning of the clause, where you will be used to seeing it in prose.

Hexameter Passage 5 *The flood abates*

Only Deucalion and his wife Pyrrha, in a little boat, have survived a flood sent by
Jupiter. At last they reach land and the flood begins to subside as Jupiter is
impressed by the couple's piety.

*The land of Phocis was once rich in fertile fields, but now it was all part of the
sea, a new expanse of water.*

mons ibi verticibus petit arduus astra duobus,
nomine Parnasus, superantque cacumina nubes.
hic ubi Deucalion (nam cetera texerat aequor)
coniuge cum cara, parva rate vectus, adhaesit,
Corycidas nymphas et numina montis adorant.   5
non illo melior quisquam nec amantior aequi
vir fuit aut illa metuentior ulla deorum.
Iuppiter, ut liquidis stagnare paludibus orbem,
et superesse virum de tot modo milibus unum
et superesse videt de tot modo milibus unam,   10
innocuos ambo, cultores numinis ambos,
nubila disiecit nimbisque Aquilone remotis
et caelo terras ostendit et aethera terris.

METAMORPHOSES I

Parnasus, -i (m.)	Parnassus (*a mountain*)
cacumen, -inis (n.)	peak
adhaeresco, -ere, -haesi, -haesum	(*here*) I come to land
Corycides, -um	of Corycus (*a cave on Parnassus*)
aequum, -i (n.)	what was right
metuens, -entis	reverent, respectful
ut	(*here*) when
stagno, -are, -avi, -atum	I am swamped
innocuus, -a, -um	innocent
ambo (acc. *ambo* or *ambos*)	both
cultor, -oris (m.)	worshipper
nimbus, -i (m.)	storm cloud

DISCENDUM *Looseness of tense*

In verse you will often see abrupt changes of tense from the past to the
historic present. This is used to add vividness to the Latin, but it can be
disconcerting to translate. So here we lurch from the perfect *adhaesit* to the
present *adorant*. Don't be confused – just find the best English (normally
keeping everything in the past).

Hexameter Passage 6 *Orpheus in the Underworld*

After his beloved wife Eurydice has been killed by a snake, Orpheus has descended into the Underworld to beg for her to be allowed to return to life. He addresses the gods of the dead, saying that even they know the power of love.

'Gods of the Dead, I have not come here to see your dark
world nor to charm your guard-dog Cerberus.'

'causa viae est coniunx, in quam calcata venenum
vipera diffudit crescentesque abstulit annos.
posse pati volui nec me temptasse negabo:
vicit Amor. supera deus hic bene notus in ora est;
an sit et hic, dubito: sed et hic tamen auguror esse,   5
famaque si veteris non est mentita rapinae,
vos quoque iunxit Amor. per ego haec loca plena timoris,
per Chaos hoc ingens vastique silentia regni,
Eurydices, oro, properata retexite fata.
omnia debemur vobis, paulumque morati   10
serius aut citius sedem properamus ad unam.
tendimus huc omnes, haec est domus ultima, vosque
humani generis longissima regna tenetis.
quodsi fata negant veniam pro coniuge, certum est
nolle redire mihi: leto gaudete duorum.'   15
METAMORPHOSES X

calco, -are, -avi, -atum	I tread on
venenum, -i (n.)	poison, venom
vipera, -ae (f.)	snake
auguror, -ari, -atus sum	I predict
mentior, -iri, -itus sum	I lie, tell a lie
rapina, -ae (f.)	abduction (*driven by love, Pluto had abducted his wife, Proserpina*)
Eurydice, -es (Gk decl.) (f.)	Eurydice
properatus, -a, -um	premature
retexo, -ere, -ui, -tum	I unravel, reverse
serius	later
quodsi	but if
venia, -ae (f.)	pardon, reprieve

DISCENDUM *The syncopated perfect and pluperfect*

In verse, the syncopated pluperfect is common, where, for example, *amaverat* becomes *amarat* (the -ve- vanishes). This also happens in the pluperfect subjunctive (*amasset* = *amavisset*) or, as here, the perfect infinitive (*temptasse* = *temptavisse*).

Hexameter Passage 7 *Scylla's terrible gift to Minos*

Minos is besieging Scylla's home city. However, overcome with love for him, Scylla betrays her country and her father Nisus by cutting off his magic lock of hair and giving it to Minos.

Scylla thought to herself, 'Why should I not be brave?
My father's magic lock will bring me what I desire.'

talia dicenti curarum maxima <u>nutrix</u>
nox intervenit, tenebrisque audacia crevit.
prima quies aderat, qua curis fessa <u>diurnis</u>
pectora somnus habet: thalamos <u>taciturna</u> paternos
intrat et (heu facinus!) <u>fatali</u> nata parentem   5
crine suum <u>spoliat</u> praedaque <u>potita</u> nefanda
per medios hostes (<u>meriti</u> <u>fiducia</u> tanta est)
pervenit ad regem; quem sic adfata paventem est:
'<u>suasit</u> amor facinus: proles ego regia <u>Nisi</u>
Scylla tibi trado patriaeque meosque Penates;   10
praemia nulla peto nisi te: cape <u>pignus</u> amoris
purpureum crinem nec me nunc tradere crinem,
sed patrium tibi crede caput!' <u>scelerata</u>que dextra
munera <u>porrexit</u>.

METAMORPHOSES VIII

nutrix, -icis (f.)	nourisher, feeder
diurnus, -a, -um	of the daytime
taciturnus, -a, -um	silent
fatalis, -e	fateful
spolio, -are, -avi, -atum	I strip (*acc.*) of (*abl.*)
potior, -iri, -itus sum (+ abl.)	I gain possession of
meritum, -i (n.)	service, benefit
fiducia, -ae (f.)	confidence
suadeo, -ere, suasi, suasum	I urge, drive one to
Nisus, -i (m.)	Nisus (*Scylla's father*)
pignus, -oris (n.)	token, pledge
sceleratus, -a, -um	abominable
porrigo, -ere, -rexi, -rectum	I stretch out

DISCENDUM *Parentheses*

Parentheses (bracketed comments) are very common in Ovid. They are usually instances of apostrophe, where the poet turns to address the reader or character, or just makes an exclamation. Don't be put off or let them get in the way of working out the main sentence.

Hexameter Passage 8 *Scylla is transformed*

When she learns that Scylla (a different Scylla to the protagonist of the previous passage) has stolen the heart of her beloved Glaucus, the witch Circe decides to destroy her rival by turning her into a monster.

Neither willing nor able to harm Glaucus, Circe turned her anger on Scylla. Having mixed a magic potion, she set off to Rhegium.

parvus erat <u>gurges,</u> curvos <u>sinuatus</u> in arcus,
grata quies Scyllae: quo se referebat ab aestu
et maris et caeli, medio cum plurimus orbe
sol erat et minimas a vertice fecerat umbras.
Scylla venit mediaque <u>tenus</u> descenderat <u>alvo,</u>   5
cum sua <u>foedari</u> <u>latrantibus</u> <u>inguina</u> monstris
adspicit ac primo credens non corporis illas
esse sui partes, refugitque abigitque timetque
ora <u>proterva</u> canum, sed quos fugit, attrahit una.
Scylla loco mansit cumque est data <u>copia,</u> primum   10
<u>in Circes odium</u> sociis <u>spoliavit</u> <u>Ulixem;</u>
mox eadem <u>Teucras</u> fuerat <u>mersura</u> carinas,
ni prius in scopulum, qui nunc quoque <u>saxeus</u> exstat,
transformata foret: scopulum quoque navita vitat.
METAMORPHOSES XIV

gurges, -itis (m.)	(*here*) pool
sinuatus, -a, -um	bowed, curved
tenus (+ abl.)	as far as, up to
alvus, -i (f.)	belly
foedo, -are, -avi, -atum	I disfigure
latro, -are, -avi, -atum	I bark
inguen, -inis (n.)	loins, private parts
protervus, -a, -um	violent
copia, -ae (f.)	(*here*) opportunity
in Circes odium	'to vent her hatred for Circe'
spolio, -are, -avi, -atum	I rob (*acc.*) of (*abl.*)
Ulixes, -is (m.)	Ulysses
Teucrus, -a, -um	Trojan (*refers to Aeneas' fleet*)
mergo, -ere, mersi, mersum	I sink
saxeus, -a, -um	made of rock

DISCENDUM *Omission of prepositions*

Prepositions, like verbs, are much more often omitted in verse than in prose. So in line 10, *loco* is best translated as '<u>in</u> this place': you need to spot the ablative and the verb *mansit* to work out that *in* + abl. is missing.

Hexameter Passage 9 *Daedalus and Icarus take flight*

Daedalus has made wings for himself and his son in the hope of escaping their captivity on Crete by air. Anxiously, he now fits the wings to his boy, warning him to be careful of the many dangers, and soon they set off.

While Icarus played with the wax and feathers, Daedalus
finished the wings and fitted them to himself.

geminas <u>opifex</u> <u>libravit</u> in alas
ipse suum corpus motaque pependit in aura;
instruit et natum 'medio' que 'ut limite curras,
Icare,' ait 'moneo, ne, si <u>demissior</u> ibis,
unda <u>gravet</u> pennas, si celsior, ignis adurat: 5
inter utrumque vola.' pariter <u>praecepta</u> volandi
tradit et ignotas umeris <u>accommodat</u> alas.
inter opus <u>monitus</u>que <u>genae</u> <u>maduere</u> seniles,
et patriae tremuere manus; dedit <u>oscula</u> nato
non iterum repetenda suo pennisque <u>levatus</u>   10
ante volat comitique timet, velut ales, ab alto
quae teneram prolem produxit in aera <u>nido</u>,
hortaturque sequi <u>damnosas</u>que <u>erudit</u> artes
et movet ipse suas et nati respicit alas.
                                                METAMORPHOSES VIII

opifex, -ficis (m.)	craftsman (*i.e. Daedalus*)
libro, -are, -avi, -atum	I balance
demissus, -a, -um	low
gravo, -are, -avi, -atum	I weigh down
praeceptum, -i (n.)	instruction
accommodo, -are, -avi, -atum	I fit
monitus, -us (m.)	warning
gena, -ae (f.)	cheek
madesco, -ere, -dui	I grow wet
osculum, -i (n.)	kiss
levo, -are, -avi, -atum	I raise myself up
nidus, -i (m.)	nest
damnosus, -a, -um	destructive
erudio, -ire, -ivi, -itum	I teach

DISCENDUM *-ere for -erunt*

As well as its use in the passive, the ending *-ere* can be added to the perfect stem to form the third person plural of the perfect active (i.e. = *-erunt*). So here *maduere* = *maduerunt* and *tremuere* = *tremuerunt*. Again, don't confuse this with the infinitive (*tremere*, etc.).

Hexameter Passage 10 *Narcissus meets Echo*

The nymph Echo has been cursed by Juno to be able only to repeat the last few words she hears, and so she is unable to express her great love for the handsome young Narcissus, who rejects her desperate advances brutally.

How often Echo yearned to speak to Narcissus and profess
her love! But Juno's curse meant she could not speak first.

forte puer comitum seductus ab agmine fido
dixerat:'ecquis adest?' et 'adest' responderat Echo.
hic stupet, utque aciem partes dimittit in omnes,
voce 'veni!' magna clamat: vocat illa vocantem.
respicit et rursus nullo veniente 'quid' inquit   5
'me fugis?' et totidem, quot dixit, verba recepit.
perstat et alternae deceptus imagine vocis
'huc coeamus' ait, nullique libentius umquam
responsura sono 'coeamus' rettulit Echo
et verbis favet ipsa suis egressaque silva   10
ibat, ut iniceret sperato bracchia collo;
ille fugit fugiensque 'manus complexibus aufer!
ante' ait 'emoriar, quam sit tibi copia nostri';
rettulit illa nihil nisi 'sit tibi copia nostri!'
                   METAMORPHOSES III

seductus, -a, -um	separated
ecquis . . .?	is anyone . . .?
Echo (Gk decl.) (f.)	Echo
acies, -ei (f.)	*(here)* gaze
totidem, quot . . .	as many as . . .
speratus, -a, -um	longed-for
collum, -i (n.)	neck
complexus, -us (m.)	embrace
copia, -ae (f.) (+ gen.)	*(here)* opportunity to enjoy

DISCENDUM *Jussive and hortative subjunctives*

The present subjunctive is often used to give a command ('may justice be done' – jussive subjunctive) or encouragement ('let us rejoice' – hortative subjunctive). Here *coeamus* is a present hortative subjunctive, meaning not 'we meet' but 'let us meet'. While this use of the subjunctive is perfectly common in prose, it is even more so in verse: look out for it and ensure you know your subjunctive endings.

Hexameter Passage 11 *Ajax stakes his claim*

Ajax argues that he, not Ulysses, should be given the arms of the late Achilles in return for his many deeds of valour in the war against the Trojans.

'I saved cowardly Ulysses' life when he was too badly
wounded to fight (though not too weak to run away!)'

'Hector adest secumque deos in proelia ducit,
quaque ruit, non tu tantum terreris, Ulixe,
sed fortes etiam: tantum trahit ille timoris.
hunc ego sanguineae successu caedis ovantem
eminus ingenti resupinum pondere fudi,   5
hunc ego poscentem, cum quo concurreret, unus
sustinui: sortemque meam vovistis, Achivi,
et vestrae valuere preces. si quaeritis huius
fortunam pugnae, non sum superatus ab illo.
ecce ferunt Troes ferrumque ignesque Iovemque   10
in Danaas classes: ubi nunc facundus Ulixes?
nempe ego mille meo protexi pectore puppes,
spem vestri reditus: date pro tot navibus arma.
quodsi vera licet mihi dicere, quaeritur istis
quam mihi maior honos, coniunctaque gloria nostra est,   15
atque Aiax armis, non Aiaci arma petuntur.'
                    METAMORPHOSES XIII

Hector, -oris (m.)	Hector (*mightiest Trojan warrior*)
Ulixes, -is (voc. *-e*) (m.)	Ulysses
ovo, -are, -avi, -atum (+ abl.)	I rejoice in, cheer at
eminus	from a distance
resupinum fundo, -ere, fudi, fusum	I knock to the ground
voveo, -ere, vovi, votum	(*here*) I pray for
Achivi, -orum (m.pl.)	Greeks
valeo, -ere, -ui	(*here*) I am successful
Danaus, -a, -um	Greek
facundus, -a, -um	eloquent
nempe	indeed
quodsi	but if
Aiax, -acis (m.)	Ajax

DISCENDUM *Poetic plural for singular*

Poetry often uses a plural noun when the singular is meant. In line 1, *in proelia* is plural (lit. 'into battles'), as is *Danaas classes* in line 11 ('Greek fleets'), but these sound rather odd in English, and so we tend to translate them just as singulars.

Hexameter Passage 12 *Apollo chases Daphne*

Apollo is in love with the nymph Daphne, but she rejects his advances. Having tried to persuade her, the god now gives chase, pursuing her through the woods.

'I am Apollo, son of Jupiter, god of prophecy, music
and medicine ... though I cannot cure my love for you.'

plura locuturum timido <u>Peneia</u> cursu	
fugit cumque ipso verba imperfecta reliquit,	
tum quoque visa <u>decens</u>; <u>nudabant</u> corpora venti,	
obviaque adversas <u>vibrabant</u> <u>flamina</u> vestes,	
et levis impulsos <u>retro</u> dabat aura capillos,	5
auctaque forma fuga est. sed enim non <u>sustinet</u> <u>ultra</u>	
perdere <u>blanditias</u> iuvenis deus, utque monebat	
ipse Amor, <u>admisso</u> sequitur vestigia passu.	
ut canis in vacuo <u>leporem</u> cum <u>Gallicus</u> arvo	
vidit, et hic praedam pedibus petit, ille salutem;	10
sic deus et virgo est hic spe celer, illa timore.	
qui tamen insequitur pennis adiutus Amoris,	
<u>ocior</u> est requiemque negat tergoque <u>fugacis</u>	
imminet et crinem sparsum cervicibus <u>adflat</u>.	

METAMORPHOSES I

Peneia, -ae (f.)	daughter of Peneus (= *Daphne*)
decens, -entis	beautiful
nudo, -are, -avi, -atum	I make bare
vibro, -are, -avi, -atum	I shake, stir
flamen, -inis (n.)	blast of wind
retro	backwards
sustineo, -ere, -ui, -tentum	I continue
ultra	further, more
blanditiae, -arum (f.pl.)	flattering words
admissus, -a, -um	(*here*) speeding
lepus, -oris (m.)	hare
Gallicus, -a, -um	from Gaul (*modern France*)
ocior, -ius	quicker
fugax, -acis	fleeing
adflo, -are, -avi, -atum	I breathe on

DISCENDUM *Split passives forms*

Notice how in verse the two parts of perfect passive verbs are often separated and scattered across the line. While in prose *aucta est* is easily translated as 'was increased', it is a little trickier when we have *aucta forma fuga est* (line 6).

Hexameter Passage 13 *Paris kills Achilles*

Apollo goes to the Trojan archer Paris, abductor of Helen; he orders him to aim for Achilles, greatest of the Greek warriors, and guides his arrow on its course.

Neptune spoke to his nephew Apollo: 'As god of archers, you should do something to stop Achilles' slaughter.'

adnuit atque animo pariter patruique suoque
Delius indulgens nebula velatus in agmen
pervenit Iliacum mediaque in caede virorum
rara per ignotos spargentem cernit Achivos
tela Parin fassusque deum, 'quid spicula perdis   5
sanguine plebis?' ait. 'siqua est tibi cura tuorum,
vertere in Aeaciden caesosque ulciscere fratres!'
dixit et ostendens sternentem Troica ferro
corpora Peliden, arcus obvertit in illum
certaque letifera derexit spicula dextra.   10
quod Priamus gaudere senex post Hectora posset,
hoc fuit; ille igitur tantorum victor, Achille,
victus es a timido Graiae raptore maritae!
                                                METAMORPHOSES XII

adnuo, -ere, -nui	I nod assent, agree to
patruus, -i (m.)	uncle (*i.e. Neptune*)
Delius, -ii (m.)	Apollo (*god of Delos*)
indulgeo, -ere, -lsi, -lsum (+ dat.)	I indulge, satisfy
Iliacus, -a, -um	Trojan
Achivi, -orum (m.pl.)	Greeks
Paris (Gk acc. *-in*) (m.)	Paris (*prince of Troy*)
fassus . . . deum	'revealing that he was a god'
Aeacides (Gk acc. *-en*) (m.)	grandson of Aeacus (= *Achilles*)
ulciscor, -i, ultus sum	I avenge
Pelides (Gk acc. *-en*) (m.)	son of Peleus (= *Achilles*)
letifer, -era, -erum	death-bringing
Priamus, -i (m.)	Priam (*king of Troy*)
Hector (Gk acc. *-ora*) (m.)	Hector (*son of Priam*)
Achilles, -is (voc. *-e*) (m.)	Achilles

DISCENDUM *Using scansion*

Scanning line 10, you will find the *-a* of *letifera* must be long (*-ā*), meaning that it is feminine ablative singular; whereas the *-a* of *certa* and *spicula* are short (*-ă*), so they must go together and be nom. or acc. (neuter plural). The feminine *dextra* must presumably also be ablative and go with *letifera*. Therefore the translation must not be 'death-bringing arrows with a sure hand', but 'sure arrows with a death-bringing hand'.

Hexameter Passage 14 *A storm at sea*

An unfortunate ship is struck by a terrible storm on the high seas and the captain is powerless in the face of nature's might.

> *The captain shouted, 'Quick, take down the yards from*
> *the top of the mast! Reef up the sails!'*

hic iubet; impediunt adversae iussa procellae,
nec sinit audiri vocem fragor aequoris ullam:
sponte tamen properant alii subducere remos,
pars munire latus, pars ventis vela negare;
egerit hic fluctus aequorque refundit in aequor,   5
hic rapit antemnas; quae dum sine lege geruntur,
aspera crescit hiems, omnique e parte feroces
bella gerunt venti fretaque indignantia miscent.
ipse timet nec se, qui sit status, ipse fatetur
scire ratis rector, nec quid iubeatve vetetve.   10
fluctibus erigitur caelumque aequare videtur
pontus et inductas aspergine tangere nubes;
et modo, cum fulvas ex imo vertit harenas,
concolor est illis, Stygia modo nigrior unda.

METAMORPHOSES XI

fragor, -oris (m.)	crash
remus, -i (m.)	oar
egero, -ere, egessi, egestum	I bail out
antemna, -ae (f.)	yard, ship's rope
indignans, -antis	angry
status, -us (m.)	state of affairs
rector, -oris (m.)	captain
erigo, -ere, -rexi, -rectum	I raise up
aequo, -are, -avi, -atum	I am level with
aspergo, -inis (f.)	spray
imum, -i (n.)	bottom, depths
Stygius, -a, -um	of the Styx (*a river of the Underworld*)

DISCENDUM *Adjectival agreement*

One of the greatest challenges of verse is piecing together adjectives and nouns in a line to find what agrees with what. Lines 7–8 here are a good example: despite the difficult word order, you need to work out that *feroces* agrees with *venti* (masculine plural nominative), and *omni* with *parte* (feminine singular ablative). You must be very focused on endings in verse and cannot rely on adjectives being next to their nouns, as they often are in prose.

Hexameter Passage 15 *Mother Earth begs for help*

With young Phaethon at the reins, the Sun's chariot careers out of control, burning the world below. Mother Earth, rising from the waters, complains to Jupiter and says she would rather be struck by his thunderbolts than suffer this.

The fish and the dolphins swam deep down to stay cool and dead carcasses of seals floated on the sea's surface.

ter Neptunus aquis cum torvo bracchia vultu
exserere ausus erat, ter non tulit aeris ignes.
alma tamen Tellus, ut erat circumdata ponto,
inter aquas pelagi contractosque undique fontes,
sustulit oppressos collo tenus arida vultus   5
opposuitque manum fronti magnoque tremore
omnia concutiens paulum subsedit et infra,
quam solet esse, fuit fractaque ita voce locuta est:
'si placet hoc meruique, quid o tua fulmina cessant,
summe deum? liceat periturae viribus ignis   10
igne perire tuo clademque auctore levare!
vix equidem fauces haec ipsa in verba resolvo';
(presserat ora vapor) 'tostos en adspice crines
inque oculis tantum, tantum super ora favillae!'
                                                          METAMORPHOSES II

Neptunus, -i (m.)	Neptune (*god of the sea*)
torvus, -a, -um	stern
exsero, -ere, -serui, -sertum	I raise out
almus, -a, -um	nourishing, fruitful
collo tenus	'as far as her neck'
infra	(*here*) lower
cesso, -are, -avi, -atum	I lie unused
auctore	'by knowing that you are its author'
levo, -are, -avi, -atum	I lighten
equidem	indeed
fauces, -ium (f.pl.)	throat
vapor, -oris (m.)	heat
tostus, -a, -um	burnt
favilla, -ae (f.)	ash, embers

DISCENDUM *Declension clashes*

There is a danger of falling into the lazy habit of piecing words together by rhyme alone (e.g. *tua fulmina* in line 9). This approach, however, will fail when dealing with words of different declensions: care is needed to see that *fracta* and *voce* agree (both ablative singular) or *tostos ... crines* or *torvo ... vultu*.

Hexameter Passage 16 *Ulysses argues for Achilles' arms*

Replying to Ajax's speech (see Passage 11), the eloquent Ulysses suggests that Ajax
would be an unworthy recipient of the weapons of the great Achilles.

'Ajax claims too much credit: it was Patroclus who
forced back the Trojans from our ships.'

'ausum etiam Hectoreis solum concurrere telis
se putat, oblitus regisque ducumque meique.
sed tamen eventus vestrae, fortissime, pugnae
quis fuit? Hector abit violatus vulnere nullo!
me miserum, quanto cogor meminisse dolore   5
temporis illius, quo, Graium murus, Achilles
procubuit! nec me lacrimae luctusque timorque
tardarunt, quin corpus humo sublime referrem:
his umeris, his inquam, umeris ego corpus Achillis
et simul arma tuli, quae nunc quoque ferre laboro.   10
sunt mihi, quae valeant in talia pondera, vires,
est animus certe vestros sensurus honores:
scilicet idcirco pro nato caerula mater
ambitiosa suo fuit, ut caelestia dona,
artis opus tantae, rudis et sine pectore miles   15
indueret?'

METAMORPHOSES XIII

Hectoreus, -a, -um	of Hector
eventus, -us (m.)	outcome
violo, -are, -avi, -atum	I injure
Achilles, -is (m.)	Achilles
procumbo, -ere, -cubui, -cubitum	I fall
tardo, -are, -avi, -atum	I delay, hinder
quin	(*here*) from ... (doing something)
scilicet	I suppose (*sarcastic*)
idcirco	it was for this reason that ...
caerula mater	'his sea-nymph mother'
rudis, -e	unrefined, brutish
induo, -ere, -ui, -utum	I put on

BONUS

1. Try scanning lines 11–12.
2. In lines 7–12, how does Ovid convey the power of Ulysses' oratory as
   he advances his case? Try to make **three** points.

Hexameter Passage 17 *Pyramus and Thisbe plan to elope*

The two lovers Pyramus and Thisbe, communicating through a crack in the wall between their houses, plan to escape at night to a place outside the city.

'Jealous wall, why do you stand in the way of our love? If
only you could let us be together . . . though we are, of course,
grateful for the crack in your surface which allows us to talk.'

talia diversa nequiquam sede locuti
sub noctem dixere 'vale' <u>parti</u>que dedere
oscula quisque suae non pervenientia contra.
postera nocturnos Aurora removerat ignes,
solque <u>pruinosas</u> <u>radiis</u> <u>siccaverat</u> herbas: 5
ad solitum coiere locum. tum murmure parvo,
multa prius questi, <u>statuunt</u> ut nocte silenti
fallere custodes foribusque excedere temptent,
cumque domo exierint, urbis quoque tecta relinquant;
conveniant ad <u>busta</u> <u>Nini</u> lateantque sub umbra   10
arboris. arbor ibi niveis <u>uberrima</u> <u>pomis</u>,
ardua <u>morus</u>, erat, gelido <u>contermina</u> fonti.
pacta placent; et lux, tarde discedere visa,
<u>praecipitat</u> in aquas, et aquis nox exit ab isdem.

METAMORPHOSES IV

pars, partis (f.)	(*here*) side of the wall
pruinosus, -a, -um	frosty
radius, -ii (m.)	ray
sicco, -are, -avi, -atum	I dry
statuo, -ere, -ui, -utum	(*here*) I decide
bustum, -i (n.)	tomb
Ninus, -i (m.)	Ninus (*an eastern king*)
uber, -eris (+ abl.)	fertile, heavy with
pomum, -i (n.)	(*here*) fruit
morus, -i (f.)	mulberry tree
conterminus, -a, -um (+ dat.)	next to
praecipito, -are, -avi, -atum	I plunge

BONUS

1. Try scanning lines 3–4.
2. In lines 10–14, how does Ovid's use of language help to paint a beautiful picture of the lovers' chosen meeting place? Try to make **three** points.

Hexameter Passage 18 *The Greeks retell their glories*

During a pause in the fighting, the Greek soldiers, in the company of Achilles, enjoy a feast and tell tales of the glories of war.

A fierce fight between Achilles and Cygnus at last came to an end.

hic labor, haec requiem multorum pugna dierum
attulit et positis pars utraque <u>substitit</u> armis.
dumque <u>vigil</u> <u>Phrygios</u> servat <u>custodia</u> muros,
et <u>vigil</u> <u>Argolicas</u> servat <u>custodia</u> fossas,
discubuere toris <u>proceres</u> et corpora <u>tosta</u>   5
<u>carne</u> replent vinoque <u>levant</u> curasque sitimque.
non illos citharae, non illos carmina vocum
longave <u>multifori</u> delectat <u>tibia</u> <u>buxi</u>,
sed noctem sermone trahunt, virtusque loquendi
materia est: pugnas referunt, hostisque suasque,   10
<u>inque</u> <u>vices</u> adita atque <u>exhausta</u> pericula saepe
commemorare iuvat; quid enim loqueretur <u>Achilles</u>,
aut quid apud magnum potius loquerentur <u>Achillem</u>?

METAMORPHOSES XII

subsisto, -ere, -stiti	I cease, stop
vigil, -ilis	alert
Phrygius, -a, -um	Trojan
custodia, -ae (f.)	sentry duty
Argolicus, -a, -um	Greek
proceres, -um (m.pl.)	chiefs
tostus, -a, -um	roasted
caro, carnis (f.)	meat
levo, -are, -avi, -atum	I relieve, lighten
multiforus, -a, -um	many-holed, perforated
tibia, -ae (f.)	flute
buxum, -i (n.)	boxwood
in vices	in turns
exhaurio, -ire, -hausi, -haustum	(*here*) I endure
Achilles, -is (m.)	Achilles

BONUS

1. Try scanning lines 5–6.
2. In lines 1–6, how does Ovid use his language to create an atmospheric account of the soldiers at rest? Try to make **three** points.

Hexameter Passage 19 *Nestor remembers Hercules*

King Nestor has just recounted the tale of the battle between the Lapiths and the Centaurs. When Hercules' son Tlepolemus asks why he did not mention his father's role, Nestor makes clear his reasons.

Tlepolemus could not contain his annoyance that his father,
Hercules, should have been passed over in silence.

atque ait: 'Herculeae mirum est oblivia laudis
acta tibi, senior; certe mihi saepe referre
nubigenas domitos a se pater esse solebat.'
tristis ad haec Pylius: 'quid me meminisse malorum
cogis et obductos annis rescindere luctus   5
inque tuum genitorem odium offensasque fateri?
ille quidem maiora fide, di! gessit et orbem
implevit meritis, quod mallem posse negare;
sed neque Deiphobum nec Polydamanta nec ipsum
Hectora laudamus: quis enim laudaverit hostem?   10
ille tuus genitor Messenia moenia quondam
stravit et immeritas urbes Elinque Pylonque
diruit inque meos ferrum flammamque penates
impulit.'

METAMORPHOSES XII

Herculeus, -a, -um	of Hercules
oblivium, -ii (n.)	forgetting, omission
senior, -oris (m.)	old man (*i.e. Nestor*)
nubigenae, -arum (m.pl.)	the Centaurs
Pylius, -ii (m.)	the king of Pylos (= *Nestor*)
obduco, -ere, -duxi, -ductum	I conceal
rescindo, -ere, -scidi, -scissum	I open up again, renew
Deiphobus, -i (m.)	Deiphobus (*a Trojan warrior*)
Polydamas (Gk acc. *-anta*) (m.)	Polydamas (*a Trojan warrior*)
Hector (Gk acc. *-ora*) (m.)	Hector (*a Trojan warrior*)
Messenius, -a, -um	of Messene (*a city in S. Greece*)
Elis (Gk acc. *-in*) (f.)	Elis (*a Greek city*)
Pylos (Gk acc. *-on*) (f.)	Pylos (*a Greek city*)
diruo, -ere, -ui, -utum	I tear to the ground, destroy

BONUS

1. Try scanning lines 2–3.
2. In lines 9–14, how does Ovid emphasize how hateful the memory of Hercules is to Nestor? Try to make **three** points.

Hexameter Passage 20 *Niobe's grief*

Niobe has insulted the goddess Latona, who therefore has ordered her children Apollo and Diana to kill all of Niobe's family. Niobe finds the corpses of her loved ones and shouts out, grieving but defiant, to Latona.

Apollo killed the last of Niobe's sons as he begged to be
saved – the wound was slight, but enough to end his life.

fama mali populique dolor lacrimaeque suorum
tam subitae matrem certam fecere ruinae,
mirantem potuisse irascentemque, quod ausi
hoc essent superi, quod tantum iuris haberent;
nam pater Amphion ferro per pectus adacto   5
finierat moriens pariter cum luce dolorem.
corporibus gelidis incumbit et ordine nullo
oscula dispensat natos suprema per omnes;
a quibus ad caelum liventia bracchia tollens
'pascere, crudelis, nostro, Latona, dolore,   10
pascere' ait 'satiaque meo tua pectora luctu!
corque ferum satia!' dixit. 'per funera septem
efferor: exsulta victrixque inimica triumpha!
cur autem victrix? miserae mihi plura supersunt,
quam tibi felici; post tot quoque funera vinco!'   15

METAMORPHOSES VI

irascor, -i, iratus sum	I am angry
Amphion, -onis (m.)	Amphion (*Niobe's husband*)
adigo, -ere, -egi, -actum	I drive, plunge
lux, lucis (f.)	(*here*) life
dispenso, -are, -avi, -atum	I give out
livens, -entis	bruised
pascor, -i, pastus sum (+ abl.)	I feed upon
satio, -are, -avi, -atum	I fill up, gorge
exsulto, -are, -avi, -atum	I rejoice
victrix, -icis (f.)	victor
triumpho, -are, -avi, -atum	I am triumphant

BONUS

1. Try scanning lines 14–15.
2. In lines 10–15, how does Ovid's use of language convey the grief-inspired defiance of Niobe's words? Try to make **three** points.

Hexameter Passage 21 *Hippomenes and Atalanta*

Atalanta, a beautiful girl and an exceptional sprinter, announces how men can try
to win her hand in marriage. Hippomenes is initially unimpressed, but when he
sees Atalanta for himself he changes his mind.

Apollo prophesied to Atalanta, 'A husband will make
you lose your own self, though you will still live.'

territa <u>sorte</u> dei per opacas <u>innuba</u> silvas
vivit et <u>instantem</u> turbam violenta <u>procorum</u>
<u>condicione</u> fugat, 'nec sum <u>potienda</u>, nisi' inquit
'victa prius <u>cursu</u>. pedibus contendite mecum:
praemia veloci coniunx thalamique dabuntur,   5
mors pretium tardis: ea lex certaminis <u>esto</u>!'
illa quidem immitis, sed (tanta <u>potentia</u> formae est)
venit ad hanc legem temeraria turba <u>procorum</u>.
sederat Hippomenes <u>cursus</u> spectator iniqui
et 'petitur cuiquam per tanta pericula coniunx?'   10
dixerat ac nimios iuvenum <u>damnarat</u> amores;
ut faciem et posito corpus <u>velamine</u> vidit,
quale <u>meum</u>, vel quale <u>tuum</u>, si femina fias,
obstipuit tollensque manus 'ignoscite,' dixit
'quos modo culpavi! nondum mihi praemia nota,   15
quae peteretis, erant.' laudando concipit ignes
et, ne quis iuvenum currat velocius, optat
invidiaque timet. 'sed cur certaminis huius
<u>intemptata</u> mihi fortuna relinquitur?' inquit
'audentes deus ipse iuvat!' dum talia secum   20
<u>exigit</u> Hippomenes, passu volat alite virgo.
                              METAMORPHOSES X

sors, sortis (f.)	(*here*) oracle
innubus, -a, -um	unmarried
insto, -are, -stiti	I urge
procus, -i (m.)	suitor
condicio, -onis (f.)	condition
potior, -iri, -itus sum	I gain possession of
cursus, -us (m.)	running race
esto! (future imperative of *sum*)	let . . . be!
potentia, -ae (f.)	power
damno, -are, -avi, -atum	I condemn

velamen, -inis (n.)	robe
meum ... tuum	*Venus is telling this tale to Adonis, a famously handsome young man.*
ignosco, -ere, -novi, -notum	I forgive
intemptatus, -a, -um	unattempted
exigo, -ere, -egi, -actum	(*here*) I consider

(a) Translate lines 1–10 (*territa ... coniunx*) into good English. **Please write your translation on alternate lines.** [30]

(b) In line 11 (*dixerat ... amores*), what does Hippomenes think about Atalanta's suitors? [2]

(c) What point do you think the story-teller (Venus) is making about Atalanta in lines 12–13 (*ut ... fias*)? [2]

(d) According to lines 14–16 (*ignoscite ... erant*), what caused Hippomenes to reconsider his opinion about the suitors? [2]

(e) Look at lines 14–18 (*obstipuit ... timet*):

  (i) write out and scan lines 16–17 (*quae ... optat*). [4]

  (ii) considering the rhythm of these lines as well as the choice and position of words, how does Ovid make clear the powerful effect Atalanta has had on Hippomenes? Make **three** points. [6]

(f) In lines 18–20 (*sed ... iuvat*), how does Hippomenes encourage himself to accept Atalanta's challenge? [2]

(g) In line 21 (*passu ... virgo*), how does Ovid's choice of words convey Atalanta's exceptional speed? Refer to the Latin in your answer. [2]

Total [50]

Hexameter Passage 22 *Alcyone's dream*

Morpheus, the god of dreams, appears to Alcyone in the form of her husband Ceyx. In this dream, Alcyone learns that her husband has died at sea, precipitating a wild outpouring of grief.

Morpheus, in the form of Ceyx, said, 'Come on, get
up, put on mourning clothes and lament my death.'

adicit his vocem Morpheus, quam coniugis illa
crederet esse sui (fletus quoque fundere veros
visus erat), gestumque manus Ceycis habebat.
ingemit Alcyone lacrimans, motatque lacertos
per somnum corpusque petens amplectitur auras   5
exclamatque:'mane! quo te rapis? ibimus una.'
voce sua specieque viri turbata soporem
excutit et primo, si sit, circumspicit, illic,
qui modo visus erat; nam moti voce ministri
intulerant lumen. postquam non invenit usquam,   10
percutit ora manu laniatque a pectore vestes
pectoraque ipsa ferit nec crines solvere curat:
scindit et altrici, quae luctus causa, roganti
'nulla est Alcyone, nulla est' ait.'occidit una
cum Ceyce suo. solantia tollite verba!   15
naufragus interiit: vidi agnovique manusque
ad discedentem cupiens retinere tetendi.
umbra fuit, sed et umbra tamen manifesta virique
vera mei. non ille quidem, si quaeris, habebat
adsuetos vultus nec quo prius, ore nitebat: 20
pallentem nudumque et adhuc umente capillo
infelix vidi. stetit hoc miserabilis ipso
ecce loco.'

METAMORPHOSES XI

Morpheus, -i (m.)	Morpheus (*god of dreams*)
illa	(*here*) Alcyone
gestus, -us (m.)	gesture, manner
Ceyx, -ycis (m.)	Ceyx (*Alcyone's husband*)
ingemo, -ere, -ui	I groan, lament
species, -ei (f.)	image
sopor, -oris (m.)	sleep
scindo, -ere, scidi, scissum	I tear
altrix, -icis (f.)	nurse

solor, -ari, -atus sum	I console
adsuetus, -a, -um	customary, normal
palleo, -ere, -ui	I am pale
umeo, -ere	I am wet

(a) Translate lines 1–10 (*adicit . . . lumen*) into good English. **Please write your translation on alternate lines.**   [30]

(b) In lines 11–12 (*percutit . . . curat*), in what **four** ways does Alcyone demonstrate her grief?   [4]

(c) In line 13 (*scindit . . . roganti*), what does the nurse do?   [2]

(d) Lines 14–17 (*nulla . . . tetendi*): how is Alcyone's reaction to the vision made particularly pitiable? Make **two** points and refer to the Latin.   [4]

(e) Write out and scan lines 18–19 (*umbra . . . habebat*).   [4]

(f) In lines 19–23 (*non ille . . . loco*), how does Ovid create a powerful picture of the wretchedness of Alcyone's husband in the dream? Make **three** points and consider the style and rhythm of the Latin.   [6]

Total [50]

Hexameter Passage 23 *Ceyx's body is washed up*

After her husband Ceyx has set out on a sea voyage, a worried Alcyone wanders
on the shore. There she sees a body washed up by the waves, but does not at first
recognize it.

Sobs interrupted Alcyone's every word, and she uttered
groans from the depths of her heart.

mane erat: egreditur tectis ad litus et illum
maesta locum repetit, de quo spectarat euntem,
dumque moratur ibi dumque 'hic retinacula solvit,
hoc mihi discedens dedit oscula litore' dicit
dumque notata locis reminiscitur acta fretumque   5
prospicit, in liquida, spatio distante, tuetur
nescio quid quasi corpus aqua, primoque, quid illud
esset, erat dubium; postquam paulum adpulit unda,
et, quamvis aberat, corpus tamen esse liquebat,
qui foret, ignorans, quia naufragus, omine mota est   10
et, tamquam ignoto lacrimam daret, 'heu! miser,' inquit
'quisquis es, et siqua est coniunx tibi!' fluctibus actum
fit propius corpus: quod quo magis illa tuetur,
hoc minus et minus est mentis, vae! iamque propinquae
admotum terrae, iam quod cognoscere posset,   15
cernit: erat coniunx! 'ille est!' exclamat et una
ora, comas, vestem lacerat tendensque trementes
ad Ceyca manus 'sic, o carissime coniunx,
sic ad me, miserande, redis?' ait. adiacet undis
facta manu moles, quae primas aequoris iras   20
frangit et incursus quae praedelassat aquarum.
insilit huc, mirumque fuit potuisse: volabat
percutiensque levem modo natis aera pennis
stringebat summas ales miserabilis undas.
                                    METAMORPHOSES XI

retinaculum, -i (n.)	mooring cable
noto, -are, -avi, -atum	I stamp, mark
reminiscor, -i	I recall
tueor, -eri, tutus sum	(*here*) I look at, see
liqueo, -ere, licui	I am clear
omen, -inis (n.)	omen, sign
vae!	alas!

propinquus, -a, -um	nearby
Ceyx, -ycis (Gk acc. -yca) (m.)	Ceyx
moles, -is (f.)	breakwater
incursus, -us (m.)	onslaught
praedelasso, -are	I dissipate, weaken
stringo, -ere, -nxi, -ctum	I graze, touch

(a) In lines 1–2 (mane . . . euntem), what does Ovid say about:

   (i) Alcyone's feelings?   [1]

   (ii) the place to which she went?   [2]

(b) Translate lines 3–12 (dumque . . . tibi) into good English. **Please write
   your translation on alternate lines.**   [30]

(c) Look at lines 12–14 (fluctibus . . . mentis):

   (i) what did the waves do?   [2]

   (ii) what was the effect of this on Alcyone?   [1]

(d) Write out and scan lines 14–15 (hoc . . . posset).   [4]

(e) Lines 16–19 (erat . . . ait): how does Ovid's use of language convey the
   power of Alcyone's grief in these lines? Make **two** points and refer to
   the Latin.   [4]

(f) In lines 19–21 (adiacet . . . aquarum), what **two** functions did the
   breakwater perform?   [2]

(g) In lines 22–24 (insilit . . . undas), how do Ovid's choice and position of
   words make Alcyone's transformation dramatic? Make **two** points and
   refer to the Latin.   [4]

Total [50]

Hexameter Passage 24 *Pygmalion falls in love*

The sculptor Pygmalion carves an ivory statue of a woman, but it is so beautiful that he falls in love with his own creation.

Pygmalion, disgusted by the immoral behaviour of women, lived alone as a bachelor for many years.

interea niveum mira feliciter arte
sculpsit ebur formamque dedit, qua femina nasci
nulla potest, operisque sui concepit amorem.
virginis est verae facies, quam vivere credas,
et, si non obstet reverentia, velle moveri: 5
ars adeo latet arte sua. miratur et haurit
pectore Pygmalion simulati corporis ignes.
saepe manus operi temptantes admovet, an sit
corpus an illud ebur, nec adhuc ebur esse fatetur.
oscula dat reddique putat loquiturque tenetque   10
et credit tactis digitos insidere membris
et metuit, pressos veniat ne livor in artus,
et modo blanditias adhibet, modo grata puellis
munera fert illi conchas teretesque lapillos
et parvas volucres et flores mille colorum   15
liliaque pictasque pilas et ab arbore lapsas
Heliadum lacrimas; ornat quoque vestibus artus,
dat digitis gemmas, dat longa monilia collo,
aure leves bacae, redimicula pectore pendent:
cuncta decent; nec nuda minus formosa videtur.   20

METAMORPHOSES X

ebur, -oris (n.)	ivory
obsto, -are, -stiti	I prevent, forbid
simulo, -are, -avi, -atum	I fabricate, pretend
insido, -ere, -sedi, -sessum (+ dat.)	I sink into
livor, -oris (m.)	bruise
blanditiae, -arum (f.pl.)	flattery
concha, -ae (f.)	shell
teres, -etis	polished
lapillus, -i (m.)	pebble
lilium, -ii (n.)	lily
pila, -ae (f.)	ball
Heliadum lacrimae, -arum (f.pl.)	beads of amber

monile, -is (n.)	necklace
collum, -i (n.)	neck
baca, -ae (f.)	pearl
redimiculum, -i (n.)	chain
deceo, -ere, -ui	I am fitting, I suit

(a) Look at lines 1–3 (*interea . . . amorem*):

   (i) how does Ovid make clear Pygmalion's abilities as a sculptor? Make **two** points. [2]

   (ii) what was the effect of such skill on the sculptor himself? [1]

(b) Write out and scan lines 4–5 (*virginis . . . moveri*). [4]

(c) Lines 4–6 (*virginis . . . sua*): how do the style and detail of these lines make clear the beautiful realism of the statue? Make **two** points and refer to the Latin. [4]

(d) Lines 6–7 (*miratur . . . ignes*): how does Ovid's language convey the impact of the statue on Pygmalion? Make **two** points and refer to the Latin. [4]

(e) Lines 8–9 (*saepe . . . fatetur*):

   (i) what does Pygmalion's infatuation lead him to do here? [2]

   (ii) what conclusion does he draw? [1]

(f) Translate lines 10–19 (*oscula . . . pendent*) into good English. **Please write your translation on alternate lines.** [30]

(g) What does line 20 (*cuncta . . . videtur*) tell us about the effect of all the adornments with which Pygmalion decorated the statue? [2]

Total [50]

Hexameter Passage 25 *Lycian peasants become frogs*

In desperate need of a drink, the goddess Latona asks some local Lycians why they will not let her and her children quench their thirst from a pool. When the peasants rudely persist in their refusal, the goddess punishes them appropriately.

As the goddess knelt down to drink from the pool, some country folk tried to stop her. She appealed to them:

'quid prohibetis aquis? usus communis aquarum est.
nec solem proprium natura nec aera fecit
nec tenues undas: ad publica munera veni;
quae tamen ut detis, supplex peto. non ego nostros
abluere hic artus lassataque membra parabam,   5
sed relevare sitim. caret os umore loquentis,
et fauces arent, vixque est via vocis in illis.
hi quoque vos moveant, qui nostro bracchia tendunt
parva sinu,' et casu tendebant bracchia nati.
quem non blanda deae potuissent verba movere?   10
hi tamen orantem perstant prohibere minasque,
ni procul abscedat, conviciaque insuper addunt.
nec satis est, ipsos etiam pedibusque manuque
turbavere lacus imoque e gurgite mollem
huc illuc limum saltu movere maligno.   15
distulit ira sitim; neque enim iam filia Coei
supplicat indignis nec dicere sustinet ultra
verba minora dea tollensque ad sidera palmas
'aeternum stagno' dixit 'vivatis in isto!'
eveniunt optata deae: iuvat esse sub undis   20
et modo tota cava submergere membra palude,
nunc proferre caput, summo modo gurgite nare,
limosoque novae saliunt in gurgite ranae.

                                        METAMORPHOSES VI

proprius, -a, -um	privately owned
abluo, -ere, -lui, -lutum	I wash
relevo, -are, -avi, -atum	I relieve
umor, -oris (m.)	moisture
fauces, -ium (f.pl.)	throat
areo, -ere, -ui	I am dry
persto, -are, -stiti, -statum	I continue
mina, -ae (f.)	threat

convicium, -ii (n.)	insult
imus, -a, -um	bottom of
gurges, -itis (m.)	(*here*) pool
limus, -i (m.)	mud
saltus, -us (m.)	jumping
differo, -ferre, distuli, dilatum	I postpone
filia Coei, filiae Coei (f.)	daughter of Coeus (= *Latona*)
supplico, -are, -avi, -atum	I beg, supplicate
stagnum, -i (n.)	pool
cavus, -a, -um	(*here*) deep
limosus, -a, -um	muddy
rana, -ae (f.)	frog

(a) Look at lines 1–3 (*quid . . . veni*):

   (i) what point about water is Latona making here? [1]

   (ii) what does she say to back up her argument? [2]

(b) In lines 4–6 (*non . . . sitim*), what does Latona say about her motivation
for seeking water? [2]

(c) Lines 6–7 (*caret . . . illis*): how do the style and content of these lines
add a tone of desperation to Latona's request? Refer to the Latin and
make **two** points. [4]

(d) Look at lines 8–9 (*hi . . . nati*):

   (i) write out and scan these lines. [4]

   (ii) what further appeal does Latona make to the peasants? [1]

   (iii) how does Ovid's use of language stress the power of this appeal?
Make **one** point and refer to the Latin. [2]

(e) In lines 10–12 (*quem . . . addunt*), how does Ovid suggest the rudeness
and intransigence of the peasants? Make **two** points and refer to
the Latin. [4]

(f) Translate lines 13–23 (*nec satis . . . ranae*) into good English. **Please
write your translation on alternate lines.** [30]

Total [50]

Hexameter Passage 26 *Phaethon drives the Sun's chariot*

Apollo, god of the sun, promised to give his son Phaethon anything he desired. Having chosen to drive the chariot of the Sun-God, Phaethon soon finds that this is not as easy or as much fun as he thought.

Apollo made his last futile entreaty: 'While you can, son, change your mind and let me drive the chariot.'

occupat ille levem iuvenali corpore currum
statque super manibusque leves contingere habenas
gaudet et invito grates agit inde parenti.
interea volucres Pyrois et Eous et Aethon,
Solis equi, quartusque Phlegon hinnitibus auras   5
flammiferis implent pedibusque repagula pulsant.
quae postquam Tethys, fatorum ignara nepotis,
reppulit, et facta est immensi copia caeli,
corripuere viam pedibusque per aera motis
obstantes scindunt nebulas pennisque levati   10
praetereunt ortos isdem de partibus Euros.
sed leve pondus erat nec quod cognoscere possent
Solis equi, solitaque iugum gravitate carebat;
utque labant curvae iusto sine pondere naves
perque mare instabiles nimia levitate feruntur,   15
sic onere adsueto vacuus dat in aera saltus
succutiturque alte similisque est currus inani.
quod simulac sensere, ruunt tritumque relinquunt
quadriiugi spatium nec quo prius ordine currunt.
ipse pavet nec qua commissas flectat habenas   20
nec scit qua sit iter, nec, si sciat, imperet illis.

METAMORPHOSES II

contingo, -ere, -tigi, -tactum	I touch
Pyrois, Eous, Aethon, Phlegon	names of the horses of the Sun
hinnitus, -us (m.)	neighing
flammifer, -era, -erum	flame-bearing
repagula, -orum (n.pl.)	barriers
Tethys, -yos (Gk decl.) (f.)	Tethys (goddess of the sea)
nepos, -otis (m.)	grandson
copia, -ae (f.)	open space
scindo, -ere, scidi, scissum	I cut
levo, -are, -avi, -atum	I lift up

gravitas, -atis (f.)	weight
labo, -are, -avi, -atum	I totter, sway
levitas, -atis (f.)	lightness
adsuetus, -a, -um	customary, normal
saltus, -us (m.)	leap
succutio, -ere	I fling about
tritus, -a, -um	well-trodden
quadriiugi, -orum (m.pl.)	team of four horses
qua	where

(a) Look at lines 1–3 (*occupat . . . parenti*):

   (i)   write out and scan lines 1–2 (*occupat . . . habenas*).   [4]

   (ii)   how does Phaethon feel? Which Latin word shows this?   [2]

   (iii)   how do Ovid's choice and position of words emphasize this feeling?
   Make **one** point.   [2]

   (iv)   how does his father feel? Which Latin word shows this?   [2]

(b) In lines 4–6 (*interea . . . pulsant*), how does Ovid convey the might of the
Sun's horses? Make **two** points and refer to the style of the Latin.   [4]

(c) In lines 7–8 (*quae . . . reppulit*), what does Tethys do, and why is she
unconcerned about doing this?   [2]

(d) In lines 9–11 (*corripuere . . . Euros*), how does Ovid paint a vivid picture
of the horses in full gallop? Make **two** points and refer to the style and
rhythm of the Latin in your answer.   [4]

(e) Translate lines 12–21 (*sed . . . illis*) into good English. **Please write your
translation on alternate lines.**   [30]

Total [50]

Hexameter Passage 27 *Cadmus becomes a serpent*

As a young man, Cadmus had slain a great serpent, sown its teeth into the ground and watched as a crop of warriors grew up from them (see Hexameter Passage 1). But now, in his old age, he is transformed into a snake himself.

As he and his wife discussed their age and misfortunes,
Cadmus recalled an event from earlier in his life:

'num sacer ille mea traiectus cuspide serpens'
Cadmus ait 'fuerat, tum cum Sidone profectus
vipereos sparsi per humum, nova semina, dentes?
quem si cura deum tam certa vindicat ira,
ipse precor serpens in longam porrigar alvum.'   5
dixit, et ut serpens in longam tenditur alvum
in pectusque cadit pronus, commissaque in unum
paulatim tereti tenuantur acumine crura.
bracchia iam restant: quae restant bracchia tendit
et lacrimis per adhuc humana fluentibus ora   10
'accede, o coniunx, accede, miserrima' dixit,
'dumque aliquid superest de me, me tange manumque
accipe, dum manus est, dum non totum occupat anguis.'
ille quidem vult plura loqui, sed lingua repente
in partes est fissa duas, nec verba volenti   15
sufficiunt, quotiensque aliquos parat edere questus,
sibilat: hanc illi vocem natura reliquit.
nuda manu feriens exclamat pectora coniunx:
'Cadme, mane teque, infelix, his exue monstris!
Cadme, quid hoc? ubi pes, ubi sunt umerique manusque 20
et color et facies et, dum loquor, omnia? cur non
me quoque, caelestes, in eandem vertitis anguem?'
METAMORPHOSES IV

traicio, -ere, -ieci, -iectum	I pierce, stab
Sidon, -onis (f.)	Sidon (*a city in the Middle East*)
vipereus, -a, -um	of a snake
vindico, -are, -avi, -atum	I avenge
porrigo, -ere, -rexi, -rectum	I stretch out
alvus, -i (f.)	belly
pronus, -a, -um	onto one's front
committo, -ere, -misi, -missum	(*here*) I unite, merge
teres, -etis	smooth

tenuo, -are, -avi, -atum	I taper
acumen, -inis (n.)	point
findo, -ere, —, fissum	I split
sufficio, -ere, -feci, -fectum	I remain
edo, -ere, edidi, editum	I utter
sibilo, -are	I hiss
exuo, -ere, -ui, -utum	I strip (*acc.*) of (*abl.*)
caelestes, -ium (m.pl.)	the gods

(a) Look at lines 1–2 (*num . . . fuerat*): what does Cadmus ponder as a possible cause of his misfortunes?   [2]

(b) Translate lines 4–13 (*quem . . . anguis*) into good English. **Please write your translation on alternate lines.**   [30]

(c) In lines 14–15 (*ille . . . duas*), what happens to Cadmus?   [1]

(d) In lines 14–17 (*ille . . . reliquit*), how is the description of Cadmus' transformation made vivid and dramatic? Make **two** points and refer to the Latin.   [4]

(e) Write out and scan lines 17–18 (*sibilat . . . coniunx*).   [4]

(f) In line 18 (*nuda . . . coniunx*), what **two** things does Cadmus' wife do which show her alarm?   [2]

(g) Lines 19–22 (*Cadme . . . anguem*):

   (i) how does Ovid's language convey the wife's horror at what is happening to her husband? Make **three** points and refer to the Latin.   [6]

   (ii) what request does the wife make at the end?   [1]

Total [50]

Hexameter Passage 28 *Medea falls for Jason*

Medea is the daughter of King Aeëtes, keeper of the Golden Fleece. When a handsome young man called Jason arrives at her father's court and is told of the many challenges he must face to gain the Fleece, Medea feels herself, against her better judgment, falling hopelessly in love with the brave traveller.

As Jason spoke to her father, Medea conceived an overwhelming love for him and could not overcome this, try as she might. She said to herself:

'frustra, Medea, repugnas:
nam cur iussa patris nimium mihi dura videntur?
sunt quoque dura nimis! cur, quem modo denique vidi,
ne pereat, timeo? quae tanti causa timoris?
excute virgineo conceptas pectore flammas,   5
si potes, infelix! si possem, sanior essem!
sed trahit invitam nova vis, aliudque cupido,
mens aliud suadet: video meliora proboque,
deteriora sequor. quid in hospite, regia virgo,
ureris et thalamos alieni concipis orbis?   10
haec quoque terra potest, quod ames, dare. vivat an ille
occidat, in dis est. vivat tamen! idque precari
vel sine amore licet: quid enim commisit Iason?
quem, nisi crudelem, non tangat Iasonis aetas
et genus et virtus? quem non, ut cetera desint,   15
ore movere potest? certe mea pectora movit.
at nisi opem tulero, taurorum adflabitur ore
concurretque suae segeti, tellure creatis
hostibus, aut avido dabitur fera praeda draconi.[1]
hoc ego si patiar, tum me de tigride natam,   20
tum ferrum et scopulos gestare in corde fatebor!'

      METAMORPHOSES VII

virgineus, -a, -um	of a virgin, virginal
concipio, -ere, -cepi, -ceptum	(5) I kindle; (10) I imagine
sanus, -a, -um	healthy

---

[1] Someone wishing to obtain the Golden Fleece had to plough a field with the fire-breathing bulls of Mars, then sow the teeth of a dragon into a field, which sprouted an army of warriors, and finally fight and kill the sleepless dragon that guarded the Fleece.

cupido, -inis (f.)	desire
suadeo, -ere, suasi, suasum	I urge
probo, -are, -avi, -atum	I approve
deterior, -ius	worse
in dis	in the gods' hands
committo, -ere, -misi, -missum	(*here*) I commit a crime
Iason, -onis (m.)	Jason
adflo, -are, -avi, -atum	I blast
concurro, -ere, -curri, -cursum (+ dat.)	I meet
seges, -etis (f.)	crop
draco, -onis (m.)	serpent
tigris, -idis (f.)	tigress
gesto, -are, -avi, -atum	I carry

(a) Look at lines 1–3 (*frustra . . . nimis*):

    (i) what does Medea say about her own resistance to her feelings? [1]

    (ii) what does she think about her father's orders? [2]

(b) Look at lines 3–4 (*cur . . . timeo*): why is Medea surprised by her own fears about Jason? [1]

(c) In lines 4–6 (*quae . . . essem*), how does Ovid's language convey Medea's mental turmoil? Make **two** points and refer to the Latin. [4]

(d) In lines 7–9 (*sed . . . sequor*), how does Ovid vividly evoke Medea's divided mind? Make **two** points and refer to the Latin. [4]

(e) Write out and scan lines 9–10 (*deteriora . . . orbis*). [4]

(f) In lines 9–11 (*quid . . . dare*), what point is Medea making? [2]

(g) How successful is Medea's attempt to resign herself to the will of the gods in lines 11–12 (*vivat . . . tamen*)? [2]

(h) Translate lines 12–21 (*idque . . . fatebor*) into good English. **Please write your translation on alternate lines.** [30]

Total [50]

Hexameter Passage 29 *Orpheus finds and loses Eurydice*

The musician Orpheus has descended into the Underworld to try to recover his dead wife Eurydice. His music persuades the powers below to allow this, until he makes a terrible mistake.

'Gods of the Underworld, if I cannot take my beloved
Eurydice back, then I too will stay here.'

talia dicentem nervosque ad verba moventem
exsangues flebant animae; nec Tantalus undam
captavit refugam, stupuitque Ixionis orbis;
tunc primum lacrimis victarum carmine fama est
Eumenidum maduisse genas, nec regia coniunx   5
sustinet oranti nec, qui regit ima, negare,
Eurydicenque vocant: umbras erat illa recentes
inter et incessit passu de vulnere tardo.
hanc simul et legem Rhodopeius accipit heros:
ne flectat retro sua lumina, donec Avernas   10
exierit valles, aut inrita dona futura.
carpitur adclivis per muta silentia trames,
arduus, obscurus, caligine densus opaca,
nec procul afuerunt telluris margine summae:
hic, ne deficeret, metuens avidusque videndi   15
flexit amans oculos, et protinus illa relapsa est,
bracchiaque intendens prendique et prendere certans
nil nisi cedentes infelix arripit auras.
iamque iterum moriens non est de coniuge quicquam
questa suo (quid enim nisi se quereretur amatam?)   20
supremumque 'vale,' quod iam vix auribus ille
acciperet, dixit revolutaque rursus eodem est.

METAMORPHOSES X

nervus, -i (m.)	string of a lyre
animae, -arum (f.pl.)	ghosts of the dead, shades
Tantalus, -i (m.)	Tantalus (*a tortured shade*)
Ixion, -onis (m.)	Ixion (*a tortured shade*)
Eumenides, -um (f.pl.)	the Furies (*avenging goddesses*)
madesco, -ere, -dui	I make wet
imum, -i (n.)	depth, lowest place
Eurydice (Gk acc. *-en*) (f.)	Eurydice

Rhodopeius . . . heros	Orpheus[1]
retro	backwards
Avernus, -a, -um	of the Underworld
adclivis, -e	steep
trames, -itis (m.)	path
caligo, -inis (f.)	darkness, gloom
margo, -inis (m.)	border, edge
certo, -are, -avi, -atum	I strive, try desperately
eodem	to the same place

(a) In lines 1–2 (talia . . . animae), what **two** actions of Orpheus caused the shades to weep? [2]

(b) Translate lines 2–11 (nec Tantalus . . . futura) into good English. **Please write your translation on alternate lines.** [30]

(c) In lines 12–13 (carpitur . . . opaca), how does Ovid's language make clear the difficulty of Orpheus' journey? Make **two** points and refer to the Latin. [4]

(d) Write out and scan lines 14–15 (nec procul . . . videndi). [4]

(e) Lines 14–16 (nec procul . . . relapsa est):

    (i)   for what **two** reasons did Orpheus look back? [2]

    (ii)   where was he at the time? [1]

    (iii) what was the effect of his turning around? [1]

(f) Lines 17–22 (bracchiaque . . . eodem est): how does Ovid fill these lines with great pathos? Make **three** points and refer to the Latin. [6]

Total [50]

---

[1] Orpheus came from the Rhodope mountains in Thrace (modern north-eastern Greece and Bulgaria).

Hexameter Passage 30 *Philemon and Baucis are rewarded*

Jupiter sends a great flood to punish a wicked neighbourhood, but saves a pious couple, Philemon and Baucis. As they watch the destruction, Jupiter asks the couple what reward they desire for their piety.

The disguised Jupiter and Mercury at last found hospitality at the house of this couple. As Philemon tried to kill their only goose for their guests to eat, the bird scuttled from reach and took refuge with the guests, who said that it should not be killed.

'di' que 'sumus, meritasque luet vicinia poenas
impia' dixerunt; 'vobis immunibus huius
esse mali dabitur; modo vestra relinquite tecta
ac nostros comitate gradus et in ardua montis
ite simul!' parent ambo baculisque levati   5
nituntur longo vestigia ponere clivo.
tantum aberant summo, quantum semel ire sagitta
missa potest: flexere oculos et mersa palude
cetera prospiciunt, tantum sua tecta manere,
dumque ea mirantur, dum deflent fata suorum,   10
illa vetus dominis etiam casa parva duobus
vertitur in templum: furcas subiere columnae,
stramina flavescunt aurataque tecta videntur
caelataeque fores adopertaque marmore tellus.
talia tum placido Saturnius edidit ore: 15
'dicite, iuste senex et femina coniuge iusto
digna, quid optetis.' cum Baucide pauca locutus
iudicium superis aperit commune Philemon:
'esse sacerdotes delubraque vestra tueri
poscimus, et quoniam concordes egimus annos,   20
auferat hora duos eadem, nec coniugis umquam
busta meae videam, neu sim tumulandus ab illa.'
                    METAMORPHOSES VIII

poenas luo, -ere, lui	I pay the penalty
vicinia, -ae (f.)	neighbourhood
immunis, -e	immune, spared from
comito, -are, -avi, -atum	I accompany
baculum, -i (n.)	staff, stick
levo, -are, -avi, -atum	(*here*) I support
furca, -ae (f.)	prop, support

stramen, -inis (n.)	straw
flavesco, -ere	I turn golden
caelatus, -a, -um	engraved
adoperio, -ire, -ui, -ertum	I cover
Saturnius, -ii (m.)	son of Saturn (= *Jupiter*)
edo, -ere, -didi, -ditum	I utter
Baucis, -idis (f.)	Baucis
Philemon, -onis (m.)	Philemon
delubrum, -i (n.)	shrine, temple
tueor, -eri, tutus sum	I tend to, serve
concors, -cordis	the same, united
bustum, -i (n.)	tomb
tumulo, -are, -avi, -atum	I bury

(a) From lines 1–2 (*di . . . dixerunt*), pick out and translate a Latin word which suggests that the gods' punishment of the neighbours will be just. [2]

(b) Look at lines 2–5 (*vobis . . . simul*):

    (i) what promise do the gods make? [1]

    (ii) Write out and scan lines 3–4 (*esse . . . montis*). [4]

    (iii) how does Ovid give the gods' words a sense of urgency? Make **two** points and refer to the style and rhythm of the Latin. [4]

(c) Translate lines 5–14 (*parent . . . tellus*) into good English. **Please write your translation on alternate lines.** [30]

(d) From lines 15–17 (*talia . . . optetis*), pick out and briefly comment on **two** details which show Jupiter's attitude to the couple. [4]

(e) Lines 19–22 (*esse . . . illa*):

    (i) what is Philemon's first request? [1]

    (ii) how does Ovid's use of language emphasize Philemon and Baucis' devotion to one another? Make **two** points and refer to the Latin in your answer. [4]

Total [50]

Hexameter Passage 31 *Argus guards Io*

Jupiter had changed his lover Io into a cow so that his wife Juno would not discover the affair; but Juno, wise to his trickery, innocently asked to have the cow as a gift. Jupiter, of course, could hardly refuse so modest a request. In this passage Juno places Io under the guard of the all-seeing Argus, forcing her to live the miserable life of a prisoner.

If he refused to give this cow to his sister and his wife, Jupiter
knew it would be revealed as more than a mere cow. So he
handed Io over to Juno.

paelice donata non protinus exuit omnem
diva metum timuitque Iovem et fuit anxia furti,
donec Arestoridae servandam tradidit Argo.
centum luminibus cinctum caput Argus habebat
inde suis vicibus capiebant bina quietem,   5
cetera servabant atque in statione manebant.
constiterat quocumque modo, spectabat ad Io,
ante oculos Io, quamvis aversus, habebat.
luce sinit pasci; cum sol tellure sub alta est,
claudit et indigno circumdat vincula collo.   10
frondibus arboreis et amara pascitur herba,
proque toro terrae non semper gramen habenti
incubat infelix limosaque flumina potat.
illa etiam supplex Argo cum bracchia vellet
tendere, non habuit, quae bracchia tenderet Argo,   15
conatoque queri mugitus edidit ore
pertimuitque sonos propriaque exterrita voce est.
venit et ad ripas, ubi ludere saepe solebat,
Inachidas: rictus novaque ut conspexit in unda
cornua, pertimuit seque externata refugit.   20
naides ignorant, ignorat et Inachus ipse,
quae sit; at illa patrem sequitur sequiturque sorores
et patitur tangi seque admirantibus offert.
                                    METAMORPHOSES I

paelex, -icis (f.)   rival (*i.e. Io*)
exuo, -ere, -ui, -utum   I lay aside
furtum, -i (n.)   crime, treachery
Arestorides, -ae (m.)   son of Arestor (= *Argus*)
Argus, -i (m.)   Argus

suis vicibus	(*here*) at a time
bini, -ae, -a	two
Io (acc. *Io*), *Ionis* (f.)	Io
pascor, -i, pastus sum	I graze (on)
collum, -i (n.)	neck
amarus, -a, -um	bitter
incubo, -are, -ui, -itum (+ dat.)	I lie on
limosus, -a, -um	muddy
poto, -are, -avi, -atum	I drink
mugitus, -us (m.)	mooing, lowing
edo, -ere, edidi, editum	I utter
proprius, -a, -um	(*here*) one's own
Inachis, -idis	of Inachus (*Io's father*)
rictus, -us (m.)	jaw
exsternatus, -a, -um	terrified
naides, -um (f.pl.)	the naiads (*river nymphs*)
Inachus, -i (m.)	Inachus

(a) Translate lines 1–10 (*paelice . . . collo*) into good English. **Please write your translation on alternate lines.** [30]

(b) From lines 11–13 (*frondibus . . . potat*), give **three** aspects to Io's life under Argus' watch which are unpleasant. [3]

(c) In lines 14–15 (*illa . . . Argo*), what problem does Io encounter? [2]

(d) In lines 14–17 (*illa . . . voce est*), how does Ovid's language evoke the wretchedness of Io's state? Make **two** points and refer to the Latin. [4]

(e) In lines 18–20 (*venit . . . refugit*), what frightens Io, and what does she do as a result? [2+1]

(f) Look at lines 21–23 (*naides . . . offert*):

    (i) write out and scan lines 22–23 (*quae . . . offert*). [4]

    (ii) how does Ovid generate pity for Io? Make **two** points and consider the style, content and rhythm of the Latin. [4]

Total [50]

Hexameter Passage 32 *Midas is punished by Apollo*

When Midas disputes Apollo's victory in a musical contest, the god punishes him with a ridiculous deformity. Although Midas tries to hide it, there is someone who cannot help but find out, and soon Midas' secret is out, albeit in an unusual way.

When Apollo played, the judge knew that he was
a class apart and urged his rival to admit it also.

iudicium sanctique placet sententia montis
omnibus, arguitur tamen atque iniusta vocatur
unius sermone <u>Midae</u>; nec <u>Delius</u> aures
humanam <u>stolidas</u> patitur retinere figuram,
sed trahit in spatium <u>villis</u>que <u>albentibus</u> implet   5
instabilesque <u>imas</u> facit et dat posse moveri:
cetera sunt hominis, partem damnatur in unam
<u>induitur</u>que aures lente gradientis <u>aselli</u>.
ille quidem celare cupit turpique pudore
<u>tempora</u> purpureis temptat velare <u>tiaris</u>;   10
sed solitus longos ferro <u>resecare</u> capillos
viderat hoc famulus, qui cum nec prodere visum
dedecus auderet, cupiens efferre sub auras,
nec posset <u>reticere</u> tamen, <u>secedit</u> humumque
effodit et, domini quales adspexerit aures,   15
voce refert parva terraeque immurmurat <u>haustae</u>
indiciumque suae vocis tellure <u>regesta</u>
<u>obruit</u> et <u>scrobibus</u> tacitus discedit <u>opertis</u>.
<u>creber</u> <u>harundinibus</u> <u>tremulis</u> ibi surgere lucus
coepit et, ut primum pleno maturuit anno,   20
prodidit agricolam: leni nam motus ab Austro
<u>obruta</u> verba refert dominique <u>coarguit</u> aures.
                          METAMORPHOSES XI

Midas, -ae (m.)	Midas
Delius, -ii (m.)	the god of Delos (= *Apollo*)
stolidus, -a, -um	stupid, unrefined
villus, -i (m.)	shaggy hair
albens, -entis	white
imas	'at the root'
induo, -ere, -ui, -utum	I assume, put on
asellus, -i (m.)	little donkey
tempora, -um (n.pl.)	temples (of the head)

tiara, -ae (f.)	turban
reseco, -are, -cui, -sectum	I cut back
reticeo, -ere, -ui	I stay silent
secedo, -ere, -cessi, -cessum	I go off somewhere, withdraw
haurio, -ire, hausi, haustum	(*here*) I dig up
regero, -ere, -gessi, -gestum	I pile back up
obruo, -ere, -ui, -utum	I bury
scrobis, -is (m.)	ditch
operio, -ire, -ui, -pertum	I cover
creber, -bra, -brum (+ abl.)	thick with
harundo, -inis (f.)	reed, rush
tremulus, -a, -um	shaking, quivering
coarguo, -ere, -ui, -utum	I expose

(a) Translate lines 1–10 (*iudicium . . . tiaris*) into good English. **Please write your translation on alternate lines.** [30]

(b) In lines 11–12 (*sed . . . famulus*), who knew Midas' secret? [2]

(c) Write out and scan lines 12–13 (*viderat . . . auras*). [4]

(d) In lines 12–14 (*qui . . . tamen*), what dilemma did this man face? [2]

(e) In lines 14–18 (*secedit . . . opertis*), how does Ovid's language dramatize the man's desperation to confess and then hide his knowledge of the secret? Make **three** points and refer to the Latin. [6]

(f) Look at lines 19–20 (*creber . . . anno*):

   (i) what appeared on the site where the man confided his secret? [2]

   (ii) when did this ripen? [1]

(g) Considering lines 21–22 (*leni . . . aures*), what does Ovid mean by *prodidit agricolam*? Explain in full. [3]

Total [50]

Hexameter Passage 33 *Ceres punishes an impudent boy*

As the distraught goddess Ceres searches for her daughter Proserpina, she relieves her thirst at the cottage of an old woman. But the woman's son teases the goddess: she, apparently lacking a sense of humour, turns him into a lizard.

The story begins:

interea pavidae nequiquam filia matri
omnibus est terris, omni quaesita profundo.
illam non udis veniens Aurora capillis
cessantem vidit, non Hesperus; illa duabus
flammiferas pinus manibus succendit ab Aetna   5
perque pruinosas tulit inrequieta tenebras;
rursus ubi alma dies hebetarat sidera, natam
solis ab occasu solis quaerebat ad ortus.
fessa labore sitim conceperat, oraque nulli
conluerant fontes, cum tectam stramine vidit   10
forte casam parvasque fores pulsavit; at inde
prodit anus divamque videt lymphamque roganti
dulce dedit, tosta quod texerat ante polenta.
dum bibit illa datum, duri puer oris et audax
constitit ante deam risitque avidamque vocavit.   15
offensa est neque adhuc epota parte loquentem
cum liquido mixta perfudit diva polenta:
conbibit os maculas et, quae modo bracchia gessit,
crura gerit; cauda est mutatis addita membris,
inque brevem formam, ne sit vis magna nocendi,   20
contrahitur, parvaque minor mensura lacerta est.
mirantem flentemque et tangere monstra parantem
fugit anum latebramque petit.
                      METAMORPHOSES V

Hesperus, -i (m.)	Evening (*the god*)
pinus, -us (f.)	(*here*) pine-torch
succendo, -ere, -ndi, -nsum	I ignite
Aetna, -ae (f.)	Mount Etna (*the gods' forge*)
pruinosus, -a, -um	frosty
almus, -a, -um	nourishing
hebeto, -are, -avi, -atum	I weaken
conluo, -ere, -ui	I wet
stramen, -inis (n.)	straw

casa, -ae (f.)	cottage
anus, -us (f.)	old woman
lympha, -ae (f.)	water
tostus, -a, -um	roasted
polenta, -ae (f.)	barley
epotus, -a, -um	drained dry
conbibo, -ere, -bibi	(*here*) I take on
macula, -ae (f.)	spot
cauda, -ae (f.)	tail
mensura, -ae (f.)	size
lacerta, -ae (f.)	lizard
latebra, -ae (f.)	hiding place

(a) Translate lines 1–11 (*interea . . . pulsavit*) into good English. **Please write your translation on alternate lines.** [30]

(b) Lines 11–13 (*at . . . polenta*): in what way did the old woman help the goddess? [2]

(c) Look at lines 14–15 (*dum . . . vocavit*):

  (i) how is the boy described? [2]

  (ii) write out and scan these lines. [4]

(d) In lines 16–17 (*offensa . . . polenta*), what was Ceres' reaction to the boy's behaviour? [3]

(e) Look at lines 18–21 (*conbibit . . . lacerta est*):

  (i) how does Ovid's use of language add drama to the boy's metamorphosis? Make **two** points and refer to the Latin. [4]

  (ii) why, according to the narrator, was the boy reduced in size? [1]

(f) How do the style and content of lines 22–23 (*mirantem . . . petit*) create a pitiable ending to the boy's story? Make **two** points and refer to the Latin. [4]

Total [50]

Hexameter Passage 34 *Arachne challenges Athene*

Arachne, a Lydian woman extraordinarily gifted at spinning, says that she could defeat the goddess of needlecraft, Athene herself, in a spinning match. Unfortunately, the disguised Athene is present as she makes such a claim.

Athene disguised herself as an old woman with grey
hair and a walking stick.

tum sic orsa loqui 'non omnia grandior aetas,
quae fugiamus, habet: seris venit usus ab annis.
consilium ne sperne meum: tibi fama petatur
inter mortales faciendae maxima lanae;
cede deae veniamque tuis, temeraria, dictis   5
supplice voce roga: veniam dabit illa roganti.'
adspicit hanc torvis inceptaque fila relinquit
vixque manum retinens confessaque vultibus iram
talibus obscuram resecuta est Pallada dictis:
'mentis inops longaque venis confecta senecta,   10
et nimium vixisse diu nocet. audiat istas,
si qua tibi nurus est, si qua est tibi filia, voces;
consilii satis est in me mihi, neve monendo
profecisse putes, eadem est sententia nobis.
cur non ipsa venit? cur haec certamina vitat?'   15
tum dea 'venit!' ait formamque removit anilem
Palladaque exhibit: venerantur numina nymphae
Mygdonidesque nurus; sola est non territa virgo,
sed tamen erubuit, subitusque invita notavit
ora rubor rursusque evanuit, ut solet aer   20
purpureus fieri, cum primum Aurora movetur,
et breve post tempus candescere solis ab ortu.
                                    METAMORPHOSES VI

ordior, -iri, orsus sum	I begin
grandus, -a, -um	great
serus, -a, -um	late
lana, -ae (f.)	wool
venia, -ae (f.)	pardon
torvus, -a, -um (understand *oculis*)	fierce
filum, -i (n.)	thread
obscurus, -a, -um	(*here*) disguised
mentis inops, inopis	weak in mind

senecta, -ae (f.)	old age
nurus, -us (f.)	(*12*) daughter-in-law; (*18*) woman
anilis, -e	of an old woman
veneror, -ari, -atus sum	I worship
Mygdonis, -idis	Lydian (*Arachne lived in Lydia*)
erubesco, -ere, -bui	I blush
noto, -are, -avi, -atum	I mark
rubor, -oris (m.)	blush, redness
evanesco, -ere, -nui	I fade
candesco, -ere	I grow white, pale

(a) Translate lines 1–11 (*tum . . . nocet*) into good English. **Please write your translation on alternate lines.** [30]

(b) In lines 11–12 (*audiat . . . voces*), what suggestion does Arachne make to the old woman? [2]

(c) Lines 13–14 (*consilii . . . nobis*): what point is Arachne making in these lines? [2]

(d) Write out and scan lines 15–16 (*cur . . . anilem*). [4]

(e) In lines 15–17 (*cur . . . exhibuit*), how does Ovid's use of language and the position of words make Athene's appearance dramatic? Make **two** points and refer to the Latin. [4]

(f) In lines 17–18 (*venerantur . . . virgo*), how does Arachne's reaction differ to that of the other women? [2]

(g) In lines 19–20 (*sed . . . evanuit*), how do we know that Arachne was embarrassed, but not for long? [2]

(h) Lines 20–22 (*ut . . . ortu*): how is this simile effective in depicting Arachne's short-lived embarrassment? Make **two** points and refer to the Latin. [4]

Total [50]

Hexameter Passage 35 *Pyramus, Thisbe and the wall*

Two next-door neighbours, Pyramus and Thisbe, fall in love, but are only able to communicate through a small chink in the wall which separates their two houses.

The story begins:

Pyramus et Thisbe, iuvenum pulcherrimus alter,
altera, quas Oriens habuit, praelata puellis,
contiguas tenuere domos, ubi dicitur altam
coctilibus muris cinxisse Semiramis urbem.
notitiam primosque gradus vicinia fecit,   5
tempore crevit amor; taedae quoque iure coissent,
sed vetuere patres: quod non potuere vetare,
ex aequo captis ardebant mentibus ambo.
conscius omnis abest; nutu signisque loquuntur,
quoque magis tegitur, tectus magis aestuat ignis.   10
fissus erat tenui rima, quam duxerat olim,
cum fieret, paries domui communis utrique.
id vitium nulli per saecula longa notatum
(quid non sentit amor?) primi vidistis amantes
et vocis fecistis iter, tutaeque per illud   15
murmure blanditiae minimo transire solebant.
saepe, ubi constiterant hinc Thisbe, Pyramus illinc,
inque vices fuerat captatus anhelitus oris,
'invide' dicebant 'paries, quid amantibus obstas?
quantum erat, ut sineres toto nos corpore iungi   20
aut, hoc si nimium est, vel ad oscula danda pateres?
nec sumus ingrati: tibi nos debere fatemur,
quod datus est verbis ad amicas transitus aures.'
                        METAMORPHOSES IV

Oriens, -entis (m.)	the East
praelatus, -a, -um (+ dat.)	pre-eminent over, superior to
contiguus, -a, -um	adjoining
coctilis, -e	made of brick
Semiramis, -idis (f.)	Semiramis (*an eastern queen*)
notitia, -ae (f.)	acquaintance
vicinia, -ae (f.)	being neighbours, proximity
taedae iure coeo, -ire, -ivi, -itum	I marry
conscius, -i (m.)	accomplice, accessory
nutus, -us (m.)	nod

aestuo, -are, -avi, -atum	I burn brightly
findo, -ere, —, fissum	I split
rima, -ae (f.)	chink, crack
paries, -etis (m.)	wall
noto, -are, -avi, -atum	I notice
blanditiae, -arum (f.pl.)	flattery, lovers' chit-chat
in vices	in turns
anhelitus, -us (m.)	panting, breathing
invidus, -a, -um	jealous
quantum erat . . .?	is it so much to ask . . .?

(a) In lines 1–2 (*Pyramus . . . puellis*), how does Ovid describe:

   (i) Pyramus? [2]

   (ii) Thisbe? [2]

(b) What **two** things do we learn in lines 3–4 (*contiguas . . . urbem*) about their houses? [2]

(c) In lines 5–8 (*notitiam . . . ambo*), what obstacle was there to Pyramus and Thisbe's love? [2]

(d) In lines 9–10 (*nutu . . . ignis*), how did the lovers first communicate? [2]

(e) Lines 6–10 (*tempore . . . ignis*): how does Ovid evoke the power of Pyramus and Thisbe's growing love? Make **three** points and refer to the style and content of the Latin. [6]

(f) Write out and scan lines 11–12 (*fissus . . . utrique*). [4]

(g) Translate lines 13–23 (*id . . . aures*) into good English. **Please write your translation on alternate lines.** [30]

Total [50]

Hexameter Passage 36 *Midas' dreadful gift*

After King Midas has reunited the god Bacchus with his tutor Silenus, Bacchus offers to give him any gift as thanks. Midas, however, chooses unwisely and soon finds out how foolish a choice he has made.

Then Midas came to Lydia and there restored
Silenus to his young ward Bacchus.

huic deus optandi gratum, sed inutile, fecit
muneris <u>arbitrium</u>, gaudens <u>altore</u> recepto.
ille male usurus donis ait 'effice, quicquid
corpore <u>contigero</u>, fulvum vertatur in aurum.'
<u>adnuit</u> optatis nocituraque munera <u>solvit</u>   5
<u>Liber</u> et <u>indoluit</u>, quod non meliora petisset.
laetus abit gaudetque malo <u>Berecyntius heros</u>
pollicitique fidem tangendo <u>singula</u> temptat
vixque sibi credens, non alta fronde <u>virentem</u>
<u>ilice</u> detraxit virgam: virga aurea facta est;   10
tollit humo saxum: saxum quoque <u>palluit</u> auro;
ille etiam liquidis palmas ubi <u>laverat</u> undis,
unda fluens palmis <u>Danaen</u>[1] eludere posset;
vix spes ipse suas animo capit aurea fingens
omnia. gaudenti mensas posuere ministri   15
exstructas dapibus nec <u>tostae frugis</u> egentes:
tum vero, sive ille sua <u>Cerealia</u> dextra
<u>munera contigerat</u>, <u>Cerealia dona rigebant</u>,
sive dapes avido <u>convellere</u> dente parabat,
<u>lammina</u> fulva dapes admoto dente premebat.   20
                          METAMORPHOSES XI

arbitrium, -ii (n.)	choice
altor, -oris (m.)	tutor (*refers to Silenus*)
contingo, -ere, -tigi, -tactum	I touch
adnuo, -ere, -ui (+ dat.)	I nod assent (to), agree (to)
solvo, -ere, solvi, solutum	(*here*) I grant
Liber, -eri (m.)	Bacchus (*god of wine*)
indoleo, -ere, -ui	I lament
Berecynthius heros	Midas

---

[1] Danae conceived by Jupiter when he appeared to her in the form of a shower of gold.

singula	'everything individually'
vireo, -ere	I am green
ilex, -icis (f.)	oak
pallesco, -ere, pallui	I turn pale
lavo, -are, lavi, lavatum/lautum	I wash
Danae (Gk acc. *-en*) (f.)	Danae
frux tosta, frugis tostae (f.)	bread (*lit. 'roasted grain'*)
Cerealia munera/dona (n.pl.)	bread (*lit. 'gifts of Ceres'*)
rigeo, -ere	I am hard
convello, -ere, -velli, -vulsum	I tear at
lammina, -ae (f.)	sheet, plate

(a) Look at lines 1–2 (*huic . . . recepto*):

   (i) what does Bacchus grant to Midas? [2]

   (ii) what is it which leads him to do so? [1]

(b) In lines 3–4 (*ille . . . aurum*), what does Midas ask for? [2]

(c) Write out and scan lines 4–5 (*corpore . . . solvit*). [4]

(d) Lines 5–6 (*adnuit . . . petisset*): pick out and translate **two** Latin words or phrases which suggest Bacchus is not optimistic about Midas' choice. [4]

(e) In lines 7–10 (*laetus . . . facta est*), how does Ovid's style emphasize Midas' great excitement? Make **three** points and refer to the Latin. [6]

(f) What test of his new power does Midas perform in lines 9–10 (*non alta . . . facta est*)? [1]

(g) Translate lines 11–20 (*tollit . . . premebat*) into good English. **Please write your translation on alternate lines.** [30]

Total [50]

Hexameter Passage 37 *The punishment of Echo*

The handsome young Narcissus rejects all his many admirers, but nonetheless the
nymph Echo cannot help but follow him, overcome with love. The curse of Juno,
however, means that she is unable to express her feelings to him.

Narcissus was sixteen years old, and he could be
considered both a boy and a man.

multi illum iuvenes, multae cupiere puellae;
sed fuit in tenera tam dura superbia forma,
nulli illum iuvenes, nullae tetigere puellae.
adspicit hunc trepidos agitantem in retia cervos
vocalis nymphe, quae nec reticere loquenti   5
nec prior ipsa loqui didicit, resonabilis Echo.
corpus adhuc Echo, non vox erat et tamen usum
garrula non alium, quam nunc habet, oris habebat:
reddere de multis ut verba novissima posset.
fecerat hoc Iuno, quia, cum deprendere posset   10
sub Iove saepe suo nymphas in monte iacentes,
illa deam longo prudens sermone tenebat,
dum fugerent nymphae. postquam hoc Saturnia sensit,
'huius' ait 'linguae, qua sum delusa, potestas
parva tibi dabitur vocisque brevissimus usus,'   15
reque minas firmat. tantum haec in fine loquendi
ingeminat voces auditaque verba reportat.
ergo ubi Narcissum per devia rura vagantem
vidit et incaluit, sequitur vestigia furtim,
quoque magis sequitur, flamma propiore calescit.   20
o quotiens voluit blandis accedere dictis
et molles adhibere preces! natura repugnat
nec sinit, incipiat, sed, quod sinit, illa parata est
exspectare sonos, ad quos sua verba remittat.
                                     METAMORPHOSES III

superbia, -ae (f.)	arrogance
trepidus, -a, -um	frightened
agito, -are, -avi, -atum	I drive
rete, -is (n.)	net
vocalis, -e	talkative
nymphe, -es (Gk decl.) (f.)	nymph
reticeo, -ere, -ui	I stay silent

resonabilis, -e	resounding
Echo (Gk decl.) (f.)	Echo
garrulus, -a, -um	chattering, talkative
deprendo, -ere, -di, -sum	I catch
prudens, -entis	clever, cunning
Saturnia, -ae (f.)	daughter of Saturn (= *Juno*)
deludo, -ere, -lusi, -lusum	I trick
mina, -ae (f.)	threat
ingemino, -are, -avi, -atum	I reduplicate
Narcissus, -i (m.)	Narcissus
devius, -a, -um	trackless
vagor, -ari, -atus sum	I wander about
(in)calesco, -ere, -lui	I grow warm (with love)

(a) Translate lines 1–10 (*multi . . . Iuno*) into good English. **Please write
your translation on alternate lines.** [30]

(b) Read lines 10–13 (*quia . . . nymphae*) and explain in your own words
what Echo used to do to annoy Juno. [3]

(c) In lines 14–15 (*huius . . . usus*), how do Ovid's choice and position
of words add power to Juno's threat? Make **two** points and refer to
the Latin. [4]

(d) *reque minas firmat* (line 16): what does Ovid mean by this? [1]

(e) In lines 18–20 (*ergo . . . calescit*), how does Ovid's use of language
convey Echo's love for Narcissus? Make **two** points and refer to
the Latin. [4]

(f) Write out and scan lines 21–22 (*o quotiens . . . repugnat*). [4]

(g) In lines 21–22 (*o quotiens . . . preces*), what did Echo desire to do? [2]

(h) In lines 22–24 (*natura . . . remittat*), what was she obliged to
do instead? [2]

Total [50]

Hexameter Passage 38 *Achilles demands a sacrifice*

The ghost of the great Greek warrior Achilles appears to his companions, reproaching them for their treatment of his corpse and demanding that a terrible sacrifice be made on his grave.

The story begins:

litore Threicio classem religarat Atrides,
dum mare pacatum, dum ventus amicior esset:
hic subito, quantus, cum viveret, esse solebat,
exit humo late rupta similisque minanti
temporis illius vultum referebat Achilles,   5
quo ferus iniustum petiit Agamemnona ferro
'immemores' que 'mei disceditis,' inquit 'Achivi,
obrutaque est mecum virtutis gratia nostrae!
ne facite! utque meum non sit sine honore sepulcrum,
placet Achilleos mactata Polyxena manes!'   10
dixit, et immiti sociis parentibus umbrae,
rapta sinu matris, quam iam prope sola fovebat,
fortis et infelix et plus quam femina virgo
ducitur ad tumulum diroque fit hostia busto.
quae memor ipsa sui postquam crudelibus aris   15
admota est sensitque sibi fera sacra parari,
utque Neoptolemum stantem ferrumque tenentem,
inque suo vidit figentem lumina vultu,
'utere iamdudum generoso sanguine' dixit
'nulla mora est; at tu iugulo vel pectore telum   20
conde meo' iugulumque simul pectusque retexit.

METAMORPHOSES XIII

Threicius, -a, -um	Thracian[1]
religo, -are, -avi, -atum	I moor
Atrides, -is (m.)	son of Atreus (= *Agamemnon*)
pacatus, -a, -um	calm
Agamemnon (Gk acc. *-ona*) (m.)	Agamemnon (*Greek high king*)
immemor, -oris (+ gen.)	forgetful of
Achivi, -orum (m.pl.)	Greeks
obruo, -ere, -ui, -utum	I bury
sepulcrum, -i (n.)	tomb

---

[1] The region of Thrace occupies modern north-eastern Greece and southern Bulgaria.

Achilleus, -a, -um	of Achilles
macto, -are, -avi, -atum	I sacrifice
Polyxena, -ae (f.)	Polyxena (*a Trojan princess*)
foveo, -ere, fovi, fotum	I warm, comfort
tumulus, -i (m.)	funeral mound
hostia, -ae (f.)	sacrificial victim
bustum, -i (n.)	tomb
memor, -oris (+ gen.)	remembering
Neoptolemus, -i (m.)	Neoptolemus (*Achilles' son*)
figo, -ere, fixi, fixum	I fix
iamdudum	at once
generosus, -a, -um	noble
iugulum, -i (n.)	throat
retego, -ere, -texi, -tectum	I uncover, bare

(a) Translate lines 1–10 (*litore . . . manes*) into good English. **Please write your translation on alternate lines.** [30]

(b) In lines 11–12 (*dixit . . . fovebat*), what does Ovid tell us about:

    (i) Achilles' companions? [1]

    (ii) Polyxena's mother? [2]

(c) In lines 12–14 (*rapta . . . busto*), what does Ovid say to arouse sympathy for Polyxena? Make **three** points. [3]

(d) How do lines 15–18 (*quae . . . vultu*) evoke a sense of foreboding about Polyxena's fate? Make **two** points and refer to the style of the Latin. [4]

(e) Write out and scan lines 18–19 (*inque . . . dixit*). [4]

(f) In line 18 (*inque . . . vultu*), what was Neoptolemus doing? [2]

(g) In lines 19–21 (*utere . . . retexit*), how does Ovid paint a moving picture of Polyxena's courage? Make **two** points and refer to the Latin. [4]

Total [50]

Hexameter Passage 39 *The death of Periclymenus*

Tlepolemus, son of Hercules, has asked Nestor why he does not praise his father. Nestor replies with a story of Hercules' terrible deeds against his family, and especially his killing of Nestor's brother Periclymenus.

'Hercules once destroyed the cities of Elis and Pylos, and ravaged my own home.'

'bis sex Nelidae fuimus, conspecta iuventus,
bis sex Herculeis ceciderunt me minus uno
viribus; atque alios vinci potuisse ferendum est:
mira Periclymeni mors est, cui posse figuras
sumere, quas vellet, rursusque reponere sumptas   5
Neptunus dederat, Nelei sanguinis auctor.
hic ubi nequiquam est formas variatus in omnes,
vertitur in faciem volucris, quae fulmina curvis
ferre solet pedibus, divum gratissima regi;[1]
viribus usus avis pennis rostroque redunco   10
hamatisque viri laniaverat unguibus ora.
tendit in hanc nimium certos Tirynthius arcus
atque inter nubes sublimia membra ferentem
pendentemque ferit, lateri qua iungitur ala;
nec grave vulnus erat, sed rupti vulnere nervi   15
deficiunt motumque negant viresque volandi.
decidit in terram, non concipientibus auras
infirmis pennis, et qua levis haeserat alae
corporis adflicti pressa est gravitate sagitta
perque latus summum iugulo est exacta sinistro.   20
nec tamen ulterius, quam fortia facta silendo,
ulciscor fratres: solida est mihi gratia tecum.'
                              METAMORPHOSES XII

Nelidae, -arum (m.pl.)	sons of Neleus
conspectus, -a, -um	fine, distinguished
iuventus, -utis (f.)	youth, young men
Herculeus, -a, -um	of Hercules
minus (+ abl.)	(*here*) except
Periclymenus, -i (m.)	Periclymenus (*son of Neleus*)

---

[1] Ovid is referring to an eagle, the bird of Jupiter.

Neptunus, -i (m.)	Neptune (*god of the sea*)
Neleus, -i (m.)	Neleus
vario, -are, -avi, -atum	I change
rostrum, -i (n.)	beak
reduncus, -a, -um	curved
hamatus, -a, -um	hooked
Tirynthius, -ii (m.)	hero from Tiryns (= *Hercules*)
nervus, -i (m.)	tendon
concipio, -ere, -cepi, -ceptum	I gain hold of, get purchase on
haereo, -ere, haesi, haesum	I stick
adfligo, -ere, -flixi, -flictum	I crash upon
gravitas, -atis (f.)	weight
iugulum, -i (n.)	throat
ulciscor, -i, ultus sum	I avenge

(a) In lines 1–3 (*bis . . . viribus*), how does Ovid convey the savagery of Hercules? Make **two** points and refer to the Latin.   [4]

(b) Look at lines 4–6 (*mira . . . auctor*):

   (i) what power did Periclymenus have?   [2]

   (ii) what reason did Neptune have to give this gift to him?   [1]

(c) Translate lines 7–16 (*hic . . . volandi*) into good English. **Please write your translation on alternate lines.**   [30]

(d) Look at lines 17–18 (*decidit . . . alae*):

   (i) write out and scan these lines.   [4]

   (ii) why did Periclymenus fall (*decidit . . . pennis*)?   [1]

(e) In lines 17–20 (*decidit . . . sinistro*), how does the style of the Latin add drama to Periclymenus' fall? Make **two** points and refer to the Latin.   [4]

(f) Lines 21–22 (*nec . . . tecum*):

   (i) what does Nestor say he does in vengeance for Hercules' brutality to his family?   [2]

   (ii) how does Nestor reassure Tlepolemus that this story will not affect their friendship?   [2]

Total [50]

Hexameter Passage 40 *Escape from Polyphemus*

Achaemenides was abandoned by Ulysses and his fellow Greeks when they fled
Polyphemus, the dreadful Cyclops of Mount Etna. Now Achaemenides, who was
subsequently rescued by Aeneas, remembers the day of his abandonment.

'May I be taken back to Polyphemus again if I ever
fail to honour and thank my saviour Aeneas.'

'quod loquor et spiro caelumque et <u>sidera solis</u>
respicio, possimne ingratus et <u>immemor</u> esse?
quid mihi tunc <u>animi</u> (nisi si timor abstulit omnem
sensum animumque) fuit, cum vos petere alta relictus
aequora conspexi? volui inclamare, sed hosti   5
prodere me timui: vestrae quoque clamor <u>Ulixis</u>
paene rati nocuit. vidi, cum monte <u>revulsum</u>
<u>immanem</u> scopulum medias permisit in undas;
vidi iterum veluti <u>tormenti</u> viribus acta
vasta <u>Giganteo</u> iaculantem saxa lacerto   10
et, ne deprimeret fluctus ventusve carinam,
pertimui, iam me non esse oblitus in illa.
ut vero fuga vos a certa morte reduxit,
ille quidem totam <u>gemebundus</u> obambulat <u>Aetnam</u>
praetemptatque manu silvas et luminis orbus[1]   15
rupibus incursat <u>foedata</u>que bracchia <u>tabo</u>
in mare protendens gentem <u>exsecratur</u> <u>Achivam</u>.
atque ait: 'o si quis referat mihi casus <u>Ulixem</u>,
aut aliquem e sociis, in quem mea <u>saeviat</u> ira,
<u>viscera</u> cuius <u>edam</u>, cuius viventia dextra   20
membra mea laniem, cuius mihi sanguis <u>inundet</u>
guttur, et <u>elisi</u> <u>trepident</u> sub dentibus artus:
quam nullum aut leve sit <u>damnum</u> mihi lucis <u>ademptae</u>!'
                                    METAMORPHOSES XIV

sidera solis, siderum solis (n.pl.)	the sun
immemor, -oris	unmindful, forgetful
animus, -i (m.)	(*here*) feelings
Ulixes, -is (m.)	Ulysses (*leader of the Greeks*)
revello, -ere, -velli, -vulsum	I tear off

[1]   Ulysses had blinded Polyphemus by driving a stake into his eye.

immanis, -e	huge
tormentum, -i (n.)	catapult
Giganteus, -a, -um	gigantic, of a Giant
gemebundus, -a, -um	groaning
Aetna, -ae (f.)	Mount Etna (*Polyphemus' home*)
foedo, -are, -avi, -atum	I befoul, stain
tabum, -i (n.)	gore
exsecror, -ari, -atus sum	I curse
Achivus, -a, -um	Greek
saevio, -ire, -ii, -itum	I rage
viscera, -um (n.pl.)	entrails
edo, esse, edi, esum	I eat
inundo, -are, -avi, -atum	I flow over
elido, -ere, -lisi, -lisum	I snap off
trepido, -are, -avi, -atum	I quiver, shake
damnum, -i (n.)	loss
adimo, -ere, -emi, -emptum	I take away, deprive

(a) In lines 1–2 (*quod ... esse*), what reasons does Achaemenides give for
his gratitude to Aeneas? [3]

(b) In lines 3–5 (*quid ... conspexi*), when does Achaemenides say he felt
truly abandoned? [1]

(c) Look at lines 5–7 (*volui ... nocuit*):

   (i) why did Achaemenides decide not to shout out? [2]

   (ii) what imperilled those on the ship? [1]

(d) Write out and scan lines 7–8 (*paene ... undas*). [4]

(e) In lines 7–10 (*vidi ... lacerto*), how does Ovid paint a dramatic picture
of the Cyclops' attack? Make **three** points and refer to the Latin. [6]

(f) Look at lines 11–12 (*et ... illa*):

   (i) what did Achaemenides fear? [2]

   (ii) why did he fear this so much? [1]

(g) Translate lines 13–23 (*ut ... ademptae*) into good English. **Please
write your translation on alternate lines.** [30]

Total [50]

An Introduction to Scansion and Ovid's Metres

Step 1: The basics

The syllable

Like English, Latin poetry is based on syllables. The difference is that English poetic metres are 'accentual', constructing rhythms from **stressed** or **unstressed** syllables:

*Once **more** unto the **breach**, dear **friends**, once **more***

Ancient poetry, however, is 'quantitative', based on length of syllable (or 'quantity') and forming its metrical patterns from **long** or **short** syllables.

Long syllables are marked   —

Short syllables are marked   ∪

Syllables which can be either long or short are marked   ×

(This is called an **anceps**.)

The foot

Poetic metres are made up of small metrical units or feet. A foot, for our purposes as readers of Ovid, can be one of two types:

Dactyl

— ∪∪	This is called a **dactyl**.
(Long – Short – Short)	*This name comes from the Greek*
'dum-di-di'	δάκτυλος *(daktylos) a finger – one long bone, two short ones.*

Spondee

— —	This is called a **spondee**.
(Long – Long)	*This name comes from* σπονδαί
'dum-dum'	*(spondai) drink-offerings to the gods,*
	reflecting the slow and stately rhythm of
	a religious ceremony.

The metres

Dactylic hexameters

The dactylic hexameter was the grandest metre of ancient poetry; it was the metre of the epic poets, greatest of whom were the Greek Homer and the Roman Virgil (a near-contemporary of Ovid). Ovid's only work in hexameters was the *Metamorphoses*.

In Greek, *hex* means six (as in <u>hex</u>agon) and *metron* is a measure or poetic foot. So the hexameter line is constituted of six feet.

A line of dactylic hexameter takes the following outline form:

$$\overset{1}{-}\overset{}{\cup\cup}|\overset{2}{-}\overset{}{\cup\cup}|\overset{3}{-}\overset{}{\cup\cup}|\overset{4}{-}\overset{}{\cup\cup}|\overset{5}{-}\cup\cup|\overset{6}{-}\times$$

In other words:

- It is made up of 6 feet.
- Feet 1–4 can be **spondees** or **dactyls**.
- Foot 5 is almost always a **dactyl**.
- Foot 6 is either long-long or long-short.

The last syllable of a line of Latin verse is always an anceps.

Elegiac couplets

With the exception of the *Metamorphoses*, all of Ovid's poetry is written in a metre called elegiac couplets. This was a very versatile metre, used by many poets, Greek and Roman, to address themes from love to war, from aetiology to lamentation.

The first, longer line of an elegiac couplet is simply a line of dactylic hexameter (see above). The second, shorter line is called a pentameter, though it is perhaps better thought of as two sets of two-and-a-half feet, rather than the five implied by *pent-*.

The pentameter line takes the following outline form:

$$\overset{1}{-}\;\overline{\smile\smile}|\overset{2}{-}\;\overline{\smile\smile}|-||\overset{3}{-}\;\smile\smile|\overset{4}{-}\;\smile\smile|\times$$

In other words:

- It is made up of 2 sets of 2½ feet:
  - Foot, Foot, long syllable; Foot, Foot, any syllable.
- Feet 1–2 can be **spondees** or **dactyls**.
- Feet 3–4 are always **dactyls**.

The double-line in the middle is called a **caesura**, and it should be marked when scanning (see Step 4 for a fuller treatment of caesurae).

* * *

Ovid, like all great poets, is master of his metre: he uses the rhythm of his lines of Latin as a powerful weapon in his poetic arsenal. In scanning lines of poetry, our aim is to identify the metrical patterns Ovid is using in order to give us a fuller appreciation of his art. For some ideas concerning the interpretations we can draw from what we find, see the chapter on *Ovid's Style* (p. 29), but ultimately it is the prerogative of each reader of Ovid to judge.

In summary, when scanning a line, the aim is to mark each syllable of the Latin in such a way that it:

- reflects the quantity (long or short) of each Latin syllable;
- gives us a pattern which fits into these outline forms.

EXERCISE 1

Practise writing out the outline patterns of the hexameter and pentameter lines. Try each three times, and then see if you can do it without looking at this book.

Step 2: The quantity of vowels

A syllable is made up of a group of letters containing a vowel. It is not always obvious (and not of pivotal importance at this stage) how a word divides into syllables, but the best arbiter is a natural sense of how a word is pronounced. It is also the case that a syllable usually starts, if possible, with a single consonant: the four syllables of *ag-ri-co-la* would be divided so (a single consonant at the start of each syllable). Of course, we can break this rule with compound words to divide them more naturally (e.g. *ob-stat*).

Now it is necessary to attempt to divine which syllables are **long** and which are **short**. For those just starting out in scansion, it is generally best to begin by trying to pick out as many obviously long syllables as possible.

A syllable is long in Latin if it is:

(i) Long by nature
    Its vowel is simply long by its nature.

(ii) Long by position
    The consonants after the vowel make the syllable long.

*   *   *

(i) Long by nature
It is not always easy to know if a vowel (and therefore the syllable) is long by nature. But here are a few naturally long vowels which are worth remembering:

-*os*, -*as*, -*es* of accusative plurals (e.g. *dominōs, puellās, regēs*);

-*a* at the end of the first declension ablative singular (e.g.
    puellā);

-*is* at the end of ablative plurals (e.g. *dominīs, puellīs*);

-u, -o and *-i* at the end of nearly all words (e.g. *annō dominī*)[1];

Diphthongs (two vowels with one sound) are also always long:
The key Latin diphthongs are: *ae* (*haec*), *au* (*aufero*) and *oe* (*poena*).

Other combinations (*ei, eu, ui*) are rarely diphthongs, but require consideration about how they are pronounced in a given word. So *huic* is one syllable (i.e. *ui* is a diphthong); but normally *ui* is not, as in *tui, sui, fui*, etc. (all two syllables, not diphthongs).

(ii) Long by position

Vowels long by position are any vowels (even if short by nature) which are 'made long' when they come before **two or more consonants.**

amavīsti, ād templum

(The two consonants do not have to be in the same word.)

However, there are **three** things to note:

a.   *x* and *z* count as double-consonants (*x* = *cs*; *z* = *ds/sd*).

   reflēxit; gāza

b.   *h* does not count as a consonant in scansion (more on this letter below), so *-ch* is counted as the single consonant *-c*.

c.   If the <u>second</u> of two consonants is *-l* or *-r* ('weak' consonants), then the vowel might still be short – the novice might do best to leave such combinations to the end when scanning.
     This does not apply to double *l* or *r*, which will make a preceding vowel long like any other two consonants.

---

[1]   Exceptions: (*-i*) *mihi, tibi, sibi, ubi, ibi* (can be long or short); *quasĭ, nisĭ* (short);
        (*-o*) *egŏ, duŏ, modŏ* (as an adverb).
   And remember, this is only for *-i* and *-o* at the <u>end</u> of a word, not in the middle.

EXERCISE 2

On the basis of the rules you have learnt in Step 2, use a pencil to mark as many long syllables as possible in these lines from Ovid's *Amores*. Remember, a syllable is marked as long with a line over it (e.g. *rēxit*). You can check your efforts on p. 190.

1. ausus eram, memini, caelestia dicere bella

2. nec sinus admittat digitos habilesve papillae

3. me legat in sponsi facie non frigida virgo

4. adspicis indicibus nexas per colla catenas

5. aptius ut fuerit precibus temptasse, rogamus

Step 3: Scanning a line

The beginner will find that the quantity of every syllable of a line of Latin will seldom be obvious, even when the information given in Step 2 has been applied. The following technique, therefore, although rather mechanical, may be useful for those taking their first steps; they can be sure that, as their confidence grows, such a formulaic approach will become unnecessary.

* * *

The hexameter line

Here is the first line of the *Metamorphoses* to practise scanning a hexameter.

> in nova fert animus mutatas dicere formas

(i) Mark in the last five syllables: essentially always |− ∪∪|−×

Mark the first syllable: it will always be long.

> in nova fert animus mutatas| dicere| formas

(ii) Next mark as many long syllables as seem obvious (e.g. diphthongs, vowels followed by multiple consonants, etc.).

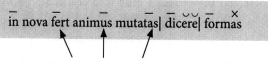

These must all be long as they are followed by two consonants.

(iii) See if that shows that any other syllables logically must be long.

Here we know that the -a- in **mut̠atas** *must be long, because after it comes a long, and then the end of the foot, so nothing but a spondee will work here.*

in nova fert animus mu|tatas| dicere| formas

This means that the -u- of **mut̠atas** *must be long as well, because short syllables always come in pairs in this metre and there is no room for a pair here.*

in nova fert ani|mus mu|tatas dicere| formas

(iv) Finally, see what is left unscanned and apply logic.

*There are two feet unaccounted for at the start of the line. There are six syllables left here (***in – no – va – fer – ta – ni***). So the missing two feet must be dactyls.*

in nova| fert ani|mus mu|tatas| dicere| formas

There it is: the first line of the *Metamorphoses* scanned.

It may sometimes be a little trickier than this, requiring even more careful logic and sometimes a little trial and error. By the way, after stage (ii), it can be helpful to count the number of syllables left: remembering that there is a maximum of 12 and a minimum of 8 syllables making up the first four feet can help in determining the number of dactyls and spondees.

The pentameter

To scan elegiac couplets, it is of course also necessary to scan the second, shorter line (the pentameter). Below is a pentameter line from Ovid's *Heroides* to practise scanning.

> quas habitas terras, aut ubi lentus abes

Again, the beginner will find it helpful to apply much the same principle as he did with the hexameter line above.

(i) Mark the last eight syllables: always $|$ $-||- \cup\cup|- \cup\cup|$ ✕

Mark the first syllable: always long.

$$\bar{} \qquad \bar{} \quad \bar{} \ \breve{}\breve{} \ - \ \breve{} \ \breve{} \ \overset{\times}{}$$
quās habitas ter|rās,|| aut ŭbĭ| lentŭs ăb|ēs

> **NB**: *The double-line (caesura) must be <u>between words</u>.*

(ii) Mark the obvious long syllables.

> *This must be long as it is followed by two consonants.*

$$\downarrow$$

$$\bar{} \qquad \bar{} \qquad \bar{} \qquad \bar{} \ \breve{}\breve{} \ - \ \breve{} \ \breve{} \ \overset{\times}{}$$
quās habitas ter|rās,|| aut ŭbĭ| lentŭs ăb|ēs

(iii) See if that shows that any other syllables logically must be long or short.

> *Here the -e- of te̱rras must be long, because short syllables always come in pairs, and there is no room for a pair here.*

$$\downarrow$$

$$\bar{} \qquad \bar{} \ \bar{} \quad \bar{} \qquad \bar{} \ \breve{}\breve{} \ - \ \breve{} \ \breve{} \ \overset{\times}{}$$
quās habi|tas ter|rās,|| aut ŭbĭ| lentŭs ăb|ēs

And that of course means the first foot must be a dactyl.

$$\overline{}\ \smile\ \smile\ \overline{}\ \overline{}\ \overline{}\ \overline{}\ \smile\ \smile\ \overline{}\ \smile\ \smile\ \times$$
quas habi|tas ter|ras,|| aut ubi| lentus ab|es

In summary, a simple and effective approach to scanning a line of Ovid's verse might be to:

i. Mark the constants at the start and end of the line;
ii. Check for obviously long vowels;
iii. See what that shows about other vowels;
iv. Use logic to work out still-unknown quantities.

EXERCISE 3

Using a pencil, try to scan the following lines. You can check your solutions on pp. 190–191.

(a) Hexameters (*Metamorphoses* I)

1.

   unus erat toto naturae vultus in orbe

2.

   ense recidendum, ne pars sincera trahatur

3.

   ignea convexi vis et sine pondere caeli

4.

   in mare perveniunt partim campoque recepta

5.

   cum sua quisque regat diverso flamina tractu

6.

   vix ita limitibus dissaepserat omnia certis

7.

   cesserunt nitidis habitandae piscibus undae

8.

vela dabant ventis nec adhuc bene noverat illos

9.

fluctibus ignotis insultavere carinae

10.

signa dedi venisse deum, vulgusque precari

(b) Elegaic Couplets (*Heroides* I)

1.

est tibi sitque, precor, natus, qui mollibus annis

in patrias artes erudiendus erat.

2.

di, precor, hoc iubeant, ut euntibus ordine fatis

ille meos oculos comprimat, ille tuos!

3.

semisepulta virum curvis feriuntur aratris

ossa, ruinosas occulit herba domos.

4.

nec mihi sunt vires inimicos pellere tectis.

tu citius venias, portus et ara tuis!

5.

quisquis ad haec vertit peregrinam litora puppem,

ille mihi de te multa rogatus abit.

Step 4: A few little extras

Is 'i' a consonant or a vowel?

The letter *i* in Latin can be a vowel or a consonant (pronounced *y* as in *y*es), so it requires a little care.[1] As usual, however, the most useful assistance will be a knowledge of how Latin words are pronounced, which most students will have obtained naturally after several years' study of the language.

For example *iussit* is pronounced as two syllables (*yus-sit*), so the *i* here is a consonantal *i* and does not count as a separate syllable (it is not *i-us-sit*). On the other hand, *filius* is pronounced as three syllables (*fi-li-us*), so the *i* here is a vowel: it is not pronounced as a *y*-sound (*fil-yus*).

When working out whether an *i* is a vowel or a consonant, it is best to trust one's instincts. Consider the following words: how many syllables do they have?

iuris	proiecit	iaciunt	impios
adicio	peior	regius	iudicis

The letter 'u'

As in English, a *u* after a *q* is not pronounced as a separate vowel, but rather together they form a *kw*-sound. So *equites* has three syllables (*e-qui-tes*); *relinquere* has four syllables (*re-lin-que-re*).

In a similar manner, and again like English, when *u* follows the combination *ng* it is not pronounced as a separate vowel, but forms a *ngw*-sound, as in 'disti<u>ng</u>uished'. So *extinguere* has four syllables (*ex-tin-gue-re*). Remember though, this is only after *ng*, not after any *g*: *exiguus* has four syllables (*ex-i-gu-us*).

---

[1] The consonantal *i* often becomes a *j* in English derivatives: so *maior* becomes *major*, *Iulius* becomes *Julius*, etc.

Elision

i. The basics

In Latin verse (as in many languages), a vowel at the end of a word does not count in scansion when the next word begins with a vowel. We say it is 'elided'.

The French, for example, do not say *je aime*, but rather the *-e* at the end of the first word is elided to give *j'aime*.

While French and Greek use an apostrophe, Latin cannot (there would be too many ambiguities of meaning) and the elided syllable will be printed. However, to reflect the fact it is elided, this syllable should be bracketed off in scanning. When spoken, this syllable was probably slurred into the next word.

PROSE		VERSE
oscula exspecto (6 syllables)	→	*oscul(a) exspecto* (5 syllables)
praeda ablata est (6)	→	*praed(a) ablat(a) est* (4)

ii. Tricky customer no.1: '-M'

If a word ends with *-am, -um, -em*, etc., then Latin counts this as a vowel in terms of scansion. Therefore, if the next word starts with a vowel, this last *-m* syllable elides.

puellam amo (5)	→	*puell(am) amo* (4)
aurum ablatum est (6)	→	*aur(um) ablat(um) est* (4)

iii. Tricky customer no.2: 'I-'

If *i* is acting as a consonant-*i* (e.g. *iussit*, where it is really a *j*), then it will not allow elision. But of course if it is a vowel-*i*, elision will occur as with any other vowel.

puella iuravit (6)	→	*puella iuravit* (6)	[*consonant-i*]
puella intravit (6)	→	*puell(a) intravit* (5)	[*vowel-i*]

iv. *Tricky customer no.3: 'H-'*

Just as French says *j'habite*, not *je habite*, so Latin does not count *h-* as
a consonant and elision will occur if the previous word ends with a
vowel/-*m*.

> *tela habeo* (5)   →   *tel(a) habeo* (4)
> *Cicero hastam habet* (7)   →   *Cicer(o) hast(am) habet* (5)

v. *A final note on 'H'*

It was noted earlier that a vowel followed by two (or more) consonants
forms a long syllable. But because *h* does not count as a consonant, it
is important to remember that if a vowel is followed by two consonants,
one of which is *h*, it could still be short.

> e.g.   *Brutŭs̲ ̲h̲abet*
>
>   ↓

u is followed by two consonants. But because one of them is an *h*,
the *u* can still be short (and here it is).

vi. *How to deal with elision when scanning*

The beginner must quickly adopt the habit of checking for and
marking elisions in a line **before** attempting to scan it. Failure to note
elision will make accurate scanning impossible.

Caesurae

A caesura (literally a 'cutting') is a break **between words but within a
metrical foot**. This is perfectly common, but every line will have one
'main caesura', where the caesura coincides with a natural break in the
Latin (often a punctuation mark) and which creates a mini-pause, a
catch of breath in the line. The main caesura should be marked with a
double line: ‖

i. Pentameters

In pentameter lines the main caesura always comes before the last seven syllables.

Main caesura

$$
\overset{1}{-}\ \overline{\smile\smile}\ |\ \overset{2}{-}\ \overline{\smile\smile}|-\|-\overset{3}{\smile\smile}|-\overset{4}{\smile\smile}|\times
$$

ii. Hexameters

The main caesura in a hexameter line will fall in the **third** or the **fourth** foot. Marked below are the four possible locations (*a–d*) of the caesura in order of likeliness (*a* = very common; *d* = very rare).

$$
\overset{1}{-}\ \overline{\smile\smile}|-\overset{2}{\overline{\smile\smile}}|-\overset{3}{\|}\overline{\smile\smile}|-\overset{4}{\|}\overline{\smile\smile}|-\overset{5}{\smile\smile}|-\overset{6}{\times}
$$
$$
\qquad a\ \ c\quad\ b\ d
$$

a – 3rd foot 'strong' caesura (*by far the most common*)
b – 4th foot 'strong' caesura (*fairly common*)
c – 3rd foot 'weak' caesura (*rare*)
d – 4th foot 'weak' caesura (*very rare*)

Here is a line of the *Metamorphoses* with its main caesura marked:

$$
\overset{-\ \smile\smile}{\text{mollia}|}\ \overset{-}{\text{cum}}\ \overset{-\ -}{\text{du}|\text{ris,}}\|\ \overset{\smile\smile}{\text{sine}|}\ \overset{-\ \smile}{\text{ponder(e),}}\ \overset{\smile\ -\ \smile\smile}{\text{ha}|\text{bentia}}\ \overset{-\ \times}{|\text{pondus}}
$$

This line has the common third foot 'strong' caesura, coinciding as so often with a punctuation mark. (Notice also the elision marked in this line.)

EXERCISE 4

You can now try to scan any line of Ovid and ask your teacher to check it. But in case you want to practise a little on your own, here are ten hexameter lines and five elegiac couplets for you to have a go at; you can check your solutions on pp. 192–193.

(a) Hexameters (*Metamorphoses* II)

1.
   ipse loco medius rerum novitate paventem
2.
   sol oculis iuvenem, quibus adspicit omnia, vidit
3.
   dixerat, at genitor circum caput omne micantes
4.
   deposuit radios propiusque accedere iussit
5.
   amplexuque dato 'nec tu meus esse negari
6.
   in promptu regere est: vix me patiuntur, ubi acres
7.
   nescius adfectas; placeat sibi quisque licebit
8.
   non tamen ignifero quisquam consistere in axe
9.
   unde mare et terras ipsi mihi saepe videre
10.
   pignora certa petis: do pignora certa timendo

(b) Elegiac Couplets (*Heroides* II)

1.
   cornua cum lunae pleno semel orbe coissent,

   litoribus nostris ancora pacta tua est—

2.

tempora si numeres—bene quae numeramus amantes—

non venit ante suam nostra querela diem.

3.

saepe fui mendax pro te mihi, saepe putavi

alba procellosos vela referre Notos.

4.

saepe deos supplex, ut tu, scelerate, valeres,

cum prece turicremis sum venerata sacris.

5.

at tu lentus abes; nec te iurata reducunt

numina, nec nostro motus amore redis.

Solutions to Scansion Exercises

Exercise 2

1. ausus eram, memini, caelestia dicere bella

2. nec sinus admittat digitos habilesve papillae

3. me legat in sponsi facie non frigida virgo

4. adspicis indicibus nexas per colla catenas

5. aptius ut fuerit precibus temptasse, rogamus

Exercise 3

(a) Hexameters (*Metamorphoses* I)

1.

ūnŭs ĕ|rat tō|to nā|tūrae| vūltŭs ĭn| ōrbĕ

2.

ēnsĕ rĕ|cīdĕn|dūm, nĕ| pars sīn|cēra tră|hātur

3.

īgnĕă| cōnvĕ|xī vīs| ēt sĭnĕ| pōndĕrĕ |caelī

4.

ĭn mărĕ| pērvĕnĭ|ūnt pār|tīm cām|pōquĕ rĕ|cēptă

5.

cūm sŭă| quīsquĕ rĕg|lăt dī|vērsō| flāmĭnă| trāctū

6.

‾ ˘˘ ‾ ˘˘ ‾   ‾   ‾ ˘˘ ‾ ˘˘ ‾ ×
vix ita| limiti|bus dis|saepserat |omnia |certis

7.

‾   ‾   ‾ ˘˘ ‾   ‾   ‾ ˘˘ ‾ ×
cesse|runt niti|dis habi|tandae| piscibus| undae

8.

‾ ˘   ˘   ‾ ˘˘ ‾   ‾ ‾ ˘ ‾ ˘˘ ‾ ×
vela da|bant ven|tis nec ad|huc bene| noverat| illos

9.

‾ ˘˘ ‾   ‾ ‾ ˘ ˘ ‾ ˘˘ ‾ ×
fluctibus| igno|tis in|sulta|vere ca|rinae

10.

‾ ˘ ˘ ‾ ‾ ˘˘ ‾ ‾ ‾ ‾ ˘˘ ‾ ×
signa de|di ve|nisse de|um, vul|gusque pre|cari

(b) Elegiac Couplets (*Heroides* I)

1.

‾ ˘˘ ‾ ˘ ˘ ‾ ‾ ‾ ‾ ‾ ˘˘ ‾ ×
est tibi| sitque, pre|cor, na|tus, qui| mollibus| annis

‾ ˘˘ ‾ ‾ ‾ ‾˘˘ ‾ ˘ ˘ ×
in patri|as ar|tes|| erudi|endus e|rat.

2.

‾ ˘˘ ‾ ˘˘ ˘ ‾ ˘ ˘˘ ‾˘˘ ‾ ˘˘ ‾×
di, precor, |hoc iube|ant, ut e|untibus |ordine| fatis

‾˘ ˘ ‾ ˘ ˘ ‾ ‾ ‾ ˘ ˘ ‾˘ ˘ ×
ille me|os ocu|los|| comprimat,| ille tu|os!

3.

‾ ˘˘ ‾ ˘ ˘ ‾ ‾ ‾ ˘˘ ‾ ˘ ‾ ×
semise|pulta vi|rum cur|vis feri|untur a|ratris

‾ ˘ ‾ ‾‾ ‾ ‾ ˘˘ ‾ ˘ ˘ ×
ossa, ru|ino|sas|| occulit| herba do|mos.

4.

‾ ˘˘ ‾ ‾ ‾ ˘ ˘˘ ‾ ˘˘ ‾ ×
nec mihi| sunt vi|res ini|micos| pellere| tectis.

‾ ˘˘ ‾ ˘˘ ‾ ‾ ˘ ˘ ‾˘ ˘×
tu citi|us veni|as,|| portus et| ara tu|is!

5.

‾ ˘ ‾ ‾ ‾‾ ˘˘ ‾‾ ‾˘˘ ‾ ×
quisquis ad| haec ver|tit pere|grinam| litora| puppem,

‾˘ ˘ ‾ ‾ ‾ ˘ ˘ ‾˘ ˘×
ille mi|hi de| te|| multa ro|gatus ab|it.

Exercise 4

(a) Hexameters (*Metamorphoses* II)

1.

    — ᴗ ᴗ   —   ᴗ ᴗ — —   ᴗ ᴗ — ᴗ ᴗ   — ×
ipse lo|co medi|us|| re|rum novi|tate pa|ventem

2.

   — ᴗ ᴗ|lis iuven — em,|| ᴗ ᴗ —   — — ᴡ   — ×
sol ocu|lis iuven|em,|| quibus| adspicit| omnia,| vidit

3.

    — ᴗ ᴗ,| —   ᴗ ᴗ   —   —   —   ᴗ ᴗ — ᴗ ᴗ   — ×
dixerat,| at geni|tor|| cir|cum caput| omne mi|cantes

4.

   — ᴗ ᴗ|it radi — os|| —   — ᴗ ᴗ ᴗ   — ᴗ ᴗ   — ×
deposu|it radi|os|| propi|usqu(e) ac|cedere| iussit

5.

   —   —   —   ᴗ ᴗ —   — ᴗ ᴗ   ᴗ ᴗ — ×
ample|xuque da|to|| 'nec| tu meus| esse ne|gari

6.

   —   —   —   ᴗ ᴗ   —   — ᴗ ᴗ — ᴗ ᴗ   — ×
in promp|tu rege|r(e) est:|| vix| me pati|untur, u|b(i) acres

7.

   — ᴗ ᴗ| adfec — tas;|| ᴗ ᴗ ᴗ   ᴗ ᴗ   —   ᴗ ᴗ — ×
nescius| adfec|tas;|| place|at sibi| quisque li|cebit

8.

   —   ᴗ ᴗ| ignife — ro|| —   —   —   — ᴗ   ᴗ   — ×
non tamen| ignife|ro|| quis|quam con|sister(e) in| axe

9.

   — ᴗ ᴗ|r(e) et ter — ras|| — —   ᴗ ᴗ   — ᴗ ᴗ   — ×
unde ma|r(e) et ter|ras|| ip|si mihi| saepe vi|dere

10.

   — ᴗ ᴗ| certa pe — tis:|| —   — ᴗ ᴗ   — ᴗ ᴗ   — ×
pignora| certa pe|tis:|| do| pignora| certa ti|mendo

(b) Elegiac Couplets (*Heroides* II)

1.

   — ᴡ   —   —   —   — ᴗ ᴗ   — ᴗ ᴗ   — ×
cornua| cum lu|nae|| ple|no semel| orbe co|lissent,

   — ᴗ ᴗ   —   —   — ᴗ ᴗ   — ᴗ ᴗ   ×
litori|bus nos|tris|| ancora| pacta tu(a) |est—

2.

¯ ∪ ∪ ¯ ∪ ∪ ¯ ∪ ∪ ¯ ∪ ∪ ¯ ∪ ∪ ¯ x
tempora| si nume|res ‖ bene| quae nume|ramus a|mantes—

¯ ∪ ∪ ¯ ∪ ∪ ¯ ¯ ∪ ∪ ¯ ∪ ∪ x
non venit| ante su|am‖ nostra que|rela di|em.

3.

¯ ∪ ∪ ¯ ¯ ¯ ¯ ¯ ∪ ∪ ¯ ∪ ∪ ¯ x
saepe fu|i men|dax‖ pro| te mihi,| saepe pu|tavi

¯ ∪ ∪ ¯ ¯ ¯ ¯ ∪ ∪ ¯ ∪ ∪ x
alba pro|cello|sos‖ vela re|ferre No|tos.

4.

¯ ∪ ∪ ¯ ¯ ¯ ¯ ¯ ¯ ∪ ∪ ¯ ∪ ∪ ¯ x
saepe de|os supp|lex, ut| tu, scele|rate, va|leres,

¯ ∪ ∪ ¯ ∪ ∪ ¯ ¯ ∪ ∪ ¯ ∪ ∪ x
cum prece| turicre|mis‖ sum vene|rata sac|ris.

5.

¯ ¯ ¯ ∪ ∪ ¯ ¯ ¯ ¯ ¯ ∪ ∪ ¯ x
at tu| lentus ab|es;‖ nec| te iu|rata re|ducunt

¯ ∪ ∪ ¯ ¯ ¯ ¯ ∪ ∪ ¯ ∪ ∪ x
numina,| nec nos|tro‖ motus a|more re|dis.

Verse Vocabulary Checklists

It has inevitably been impossible to pitch the level of vocabulary in such a way that it meets all needs. Some will find this list too extensive, others too limited. Nevertheless it is hoped that these 450 items of vocabulary will constitute a useful suggested list of the most common words which recur in Ovid and which will, for the most part, be new to the first-time reader.

Words are not included in this list if:

(a) they are likely to be known by students who are competent enough to attempt unseen verse (I have used the word lists provided by various examination boards for AS/A2 Level to gauge this);

(b) they should be easily deducible by context or English derivatives;

(c) they are relatively rare, and have therefore been glossed.

Some of the words in these checklists are still glossed beneath the early passages, to allow readers some leeway in accustoming themselves to these new words.

Before beginning the first passage, it will be worth the student's while to learn the Fifty Verse Starter Words below: these include some very common words, knowledge of which is assumed from Passage 1 onwards.

The remaining 400 words are broken down into ten checklists of roughly equal length. Each Checklist corresponds to a group of four passages, both Elegiac and Hexameter, and includes new words encountered in them (so Checklist 1 has the new vocabulary from Elegiac Passages 1–4 **and** Hexameter Passages 1–4; Checklist 2 from both sets of Passages 5–8, etc.). In this way the student is developing a broader verse vocabulary than simply the new words in the passages from the half he is reading.

FIFTY VERSE STARTER WORDS

aequor, -oris (*n.*)	sea
aer, aeris (*Gk acc.* aera) (*m.*)	air
aether, -eris (*Gk acc.* aethera) (*m.*)	air, sky
astrum, -i (*n.*)	star, constellation
aura, -ae (*f.*)	breeze, air
bracchium, -ii (*n.*)	arm
caelestis, -e	heavenly, divine
candidus, -a, -um	white, bright
capillus, -i (*m.*) (*usually plural*)	hair
color, -oris (*m.*)	colour, complexion
coma, -ae (*f.*)	hair
cresco, -ere, crevi, cretum	I increase, grow, arise
dictum, -i (*n.*)	word
dulcis, -e	sweet, pleasant
ensis, -is (*m.*)	sword
exiguus, -a, -um	small
ferio, -ire	I strike, hit
fretum, -i (*n.*)	strait, sea
genu, -us (*n.*)	knee
Iuppiter, Iovis (*m.*)	Jupiter (*king of the gods*)
lanio, -are, -avi, -atum	I tear (at)
lectus, -i (*m.*)	bed, couch
leniter	gently, softly
lumen, -inis (*n.*)	light, lamp; eye
maestus, -a, -um	sad, gloomy
Mars, Martis (*m.*)	Mars (*god of war*); war
mirus, -a, -um	wonderful, marvellous, amazing

mitis, -e	soft, gentle
mollis, -e	soft, gentle
nata, -ae (*f.*)/natus, -i (*m.*)	daughter/son
nubes, -is (*f.*)	cloud
orbis, -is (*m.*)	sphere; world, country; eye
Pallas, -adis (*Gk acc.* Pallada) (*f.*)	Pallas Athene (*goddess of wisdom*)
pavidus, -a, -um	trembling, terrified, alarmed
pectus, -oris (*n.*)	breast, chest, heart
penna, -ae (*f.*)	feather; (*plural*) wing
pietas, -atis (*f.*)	devotion, piety
protinus	on the spot, immediately
puppis, -is (*f.*)	stern, ship
quid?	what?; why?
saucius, -a, -um	wounded
stupeo, -ere, stupui	I am amazed, dumbstruck
taurus, -i (*m.*)	bull
tellus, -uris (*f.*)	land, earth
tenuis, -e	thin, slender, weak
tepidus, -a, -um	warm
ter	three times
tremo, -ere, -ui	I shake, tremble (at)
vela, -orum (*n.pl.*)	sails
virgo, -inis (*f.*)	girl, maiden

VOCABULARY CHECKLIST 1 (Elegiac and Hexameter Passages 1–4)

agna, -ae (*f.*)	lamb
agnus, -i (*m.*)	lamb
amplexus, -us (*m.*)	embrace
aratrum, -i (*n.*)	plough
auctor, -oris (*m.*)	author, originator, do-er; father
axis, -is (*m.*)	vault of heaven; axle, chariot

careo, -ere, carui (+ *abl.*)	I lack, am without
columba, -ae (*f.*)	dove
creo, -are, creavi, creatum	I create, make, give birth to
crinis, -is (*m.*)	hair
(re)curvus, -a, -um	hooked, curved
-cutio, -ere, -cussi, -cussum	I shake, strike (*in compounds*)
desero, -ere, -ui, -sertum	I abandon, forsake
furo, -ere	I rage, am frenzied; I rush
gelidus, -a, -um	icy, cold, frozen
geminus, -a, -um	twin, double; (*plural*) both
horreo, -ere, -ui	I bristle; I shudder at, fear
letum, -i (*n.*)	death
lupa, -ae (*f.*)	she-wolf
lupus, -i (*m.*)	wolf
nefandus, -a, -um	accursed, evil, wicked
nequeo, -ire, -ivi	I am unable
pariter	together, at the same time
pateo, -ere, -ui	I lie open, am clear
Penates, -ium (*m.pl.*)	household gods; home
perdo, -ere, -didi, -ditum	I destroy, ruin; I lose, waste
purpureus, -a, -um	purple; radiant, glowing
salio, -ire, salui, saltum	I jump, leap
(*compounds* -silio)	
sanguineus, -a, -um	bloody, of blood, blood-red
seges, -etis (*f.*)	corn, crop
serpens, -entis (*m.*)	snake, dragon
sinus, -us (*m.*)	bosom, lap; bay; fold
spargo, -ere, -rsi, -rsum	I scatter, sprinkle
spiro, -are, -avi, -atum	I breathe, blow; I am alive
exspiro, -are, -avi, -atum	I breathe out; I expire
sublimis, -e	on high, lofty
superus, -a, -um	high, above

tendo, -ere, tetendi, tentum	I stretch out; I head for, aim
thalamus, -i (*m.*)	bed-chamber
tono, -are, tonui, tonitum	I thunder
torus, -i (*m.*)	bed, couch, marriage-bed
umerus, -i (*m.*)	shoulder
velo, -are, -avi, -atum	I cover, clothe, conceal

VOCABULARY CHECKLIST 2 (Elegiac and Hexameter Passages 5–8)

adfor, -fari, -fatus sum	I address
aestus, -us (*m.*)	heat; surging sea; passion
Aquilo, -onis (*m.*)	North wind
arcus, -us (*m.*)	bow; curve
arduus, -a, -um	high, steep; difficult
caedo, -ere, cecidi, caesum	I slaughter, kill
carina, -ae (*f.*)	boat, ship
carpo, -ere, -psi, -ptum	I pluck; (*of a road*) I take
citus, -a, -um	quick, swift, rapid
citius (*comparative adverb*)	more quickly
cito (*adverb*)	quickly
fateor, -eri, fassus sum	I confess, acknowledge
fatum, -i (*n.*)	fate
heu!	alas!
iacto, -are, -avi, -atum	I toss about, hurl; I boast
liquidus, -a, -um	clear
meritus, -a, -um	deserving; deserved
meritum, -i (*n.*)	deserts, what one deserves
monstrum, -i (*n.*)	monster
mortalis, -e	mortal, human
navita, -ae (*m.*)	sailor (= *nauta*)
no, nare, navi	I swim (*often in compounds*)

nubilus, -a, -um	cloudy
nubila, -orum (*n.pl.*)	clouds
numen, -inis (*n.*)	divinity, divine power; god
nympha/-e, -ae (*f.*)	nymph; young woman, bride
[ops,] opis (*f.*)	help; power
opes, -um (*f.pl.*)	resources, wealth
palus, -udis (*f.*)	marsh, pool
paternus, -a, -um	of one's father; ancestral
patrius, -a, -um	of one's father; ancestral
paveo, -ere, pavi	I am struck with fear
proles, -is (*f.*)	offspring, child, descendant
propero, -are, -avi, -atum	I hurry, am quick
ratis, -is (*f.*)	boat
regius, -a, -um	royal
scopulus, -i (*m.*)	rock, cliff
sidereus, -a, -um	starry
subeo, -ire, -i(v)i, -itum	I go under, approach; I come to mind
tempto, -are, -avi, -atum	I handle, touch; I try, attempt
tenebrae, -arum (*f.pl.*)	darkness, night
timidus, -a, -um	fearful, faint-hearted
vastus, -a, -um	enormous, vast
vertex, -icis (*m.*)	summit, peak; whirlpool

VOCABULARY CHECKLIST 3 (Elegiac and Hexameter Passages 9–12)

aeger, aegra, aegrum	sick, weary; love-sick
aegre	with difficulty
ait (*plural* aiunt)	(s)he says, said; they say, said
ala, -ae (*f.*)	wing
ales, alitis	winged; (*as a noun*) bird
amica, -ae (*f.*)	girlfriend

antiquus, -a, -um	ancient, previous
aptus, -a, -um	suitable, appropriate
arvum, -i (*n.*)	field, land
celsus, -a, -um	high, lofty
cervix, -icis (*f.*)	neck
classis, -is (*f.*)	fleet
corona, -ae (*f.*)	wreath, garland, crown
diligo, -ere, dilexi, dilectum	I love
fidus, -a, -um	trusty
forma, -ae (*f.*)	form, shape; beauty
fulgeo, -ere, fulsi	I flash, gleam, shine
harena, -ae (*f.*)	sand; arena, amphitheatre
hesternus, -a, -um	of yesterday
immineo, -ere	I threaten, hang over; I follow close
lacertus, -i (*m.*)	arm, upper arm; embrace
lassatus, -a, -um	weary, tired
lassus, -a, -um	weary, tired
limes, -itis (*m.*)	boundary, track
nudus, -a, -um	naked, bare
pendo, -ere, pependi, pensum	I hang, suspend; I weigh
pondus, -eris (*n.*)	weight
preces, -um (*f.pl.*)	prayers
premo, -ere, pressi, pressum	I press, press on; I crush
quamvis	although
regia, -ae (*f.*)	palace
requies, -etis (*f.*)	rest, respite
rivus, -i (*m.*)	stream
sacrum, -i (*n.*)	religious rite, ceremony (*often pl.*)
senilis, -e	of an old man
singuli, -ae, -a (*pl.*)	one each, individual

somnium, -ii (*n.*)	dream
sors, sortis (*f.*)	lot, share, fortune
tener, -era, -erum	soft, delicate, tender
tunica, -ae (*f.*)	dress
uro, -ere, ussi, ustum	I burn
ventosus, -a, -um	windy
Venus, -eris (*f.*)	Venus (*goddess of love*); love
vestigium, -ii (*n.*)	footstep; trace
volo, -are, -avi, -atum	I fly

VOCABULARY CHECKLIST 4 (Elegiac and Hexameter Passages 13–16)

asper, -era, -erum	harsh, cruel; ruinous
Boreas, -eae (*Gk acc.* -an) (*m.*)	North wind
castus, -a, -um	chaste, virtuous
cerno, -ere, crevi, cretum	I look at, see; I decide
diva, -ae (*f.*)	goddess
divus, -i (*m.*)	god
en!	Lo! Look!
ferus, -a, -um	wild, savage, cruel
fluctus, -us (*m.*)	wave, flood
frons, frontis (*f.*)	forehead, brow; front
fulmen, -inis (*n.*)	lightning, thunderbolt
fulvus, -a, -um	golden, tawny
Graius, -a, -um	Greek
imago, -inis (*f.*)	image, likeness; ghost
imber, imbris (*m.*)	rain, shower
Iuno, -onis (*f.*)	Juno (*queen of the gods*)
luctus, -us (*m.*)	grief, sorrow, mourning
mereo, -ere, -ui, -itum	I deserve
minister, -tri (*m.*)	servant
misceo, -ere, miscui, mixtum	I mix, confuse

modo . . . modo . . .	at one time . . . at another . . .
nebula, -ae (*f.*)	cloud
niger, -ra, -rum	black
nitor, -i, nisus/nixus sum	I rest, lean on; I climb, strive
Notus, -i (*m.*)	South wind; wind
ovis, -is (*f.*)	sheep
pelagus, -i (*n.*)	open sea
pontus, -i (*m.*)	sea
procella, -ae (*f.*)	storm, gale
rarus, -a, -um	rare, occasional, spread out
spiculum, -i (*n.*)	arrow, dart
sterno, -ere, stravi, stratum	I lay low, kill; I spread, lay out
subitus, -a, -um	sudden
tremor, -oris (*m.*)	shaking, trembling; earthquake
Troicus, -a, -um	Trojan
velox, velocis	swift, quick
vinc(u)lum, -i (*n.*)	fastening, rope, chain
vomer, -eris (*n.*)	ploughshare, plough

VOCABULARY CHECKLIST 5 (Elegiac and Hexameter Passages 17–20)

Aurora, -ae (*f.*)	(goddess of) Dawn
avis, -is (*f.*)	bird
bos, bovis (*c.*)	ox, cow
cithara, -ae (*f.*)	lyre
cor, cordis (*n.*)	heart
-cumbo, -ere, -cubui, -cubitum	I lie, fall (*in compounds*)
decet, -ere, -uit (*impers.*)	it is fitting, right, decent
delecto, -are, -avi, -atum	I delight, amuse
domo, -are, -ui, -itum	I subdue, overcome
facies, -ei (*f.*)	shape, appearance; face
figura, -ae (*f.*)	shape, figure, form, image

fores, -ium (*f.pl.*)	door
funus, -eris (*n.*)	funeral, death
genitor, -oris (*m.*)	father
glacies, -ei (*f.*)	ice
gratus, -a, -um	welcome, pleasing
herba, -ae (*f.*)	grass; herb
immeritus, -a, -um	undeserving; undeserved
iugum, -i (*n.*)	yoke; mountain ridge
iuvo, -are, iuvi, iutum	I help; I am pleasing
iuvat (*impers.*)	it is pleasing
lateo, -ere, -ui	I lie hidden
nequiquam	in vain
niveus, -a, -um	snowy, white
nocturnus, -a, -um	nocturnal, of the night
orbus, -a, -um	deprived, bereft (of, + *abl.*)
osculum, -i (*n.*)	kiss
pactus, -a, -um	agreed, settled
-pleo, -ere, -plevi, -pletum	I fill (*in compounds*)
polus, -i (*m.*)	pole; sky, heaven
ruina, -ae (*f.*)	fall, ruin, destruction
sileo, -ere, silui	I am silent, am still
sitis, -is (*acc.* -im) (*f.*)	thirst
superi, -orum (*m.pl.*)	gods
supremus, -a, -um	highest; last
tardus, -a, -um	slow, delaying
triumphus, -i (*m.*)	triumph
Troia, -ae (*f.*)	Troy
turpis, -e	ugly, shameful, disgraceful
vacca, -ae (*f.*)	cow
votum, -i (*n.*)	vow, promise, wish, prayer

VOCABULARY CHECKLIST 6 (Elegiac and Hexameter Passages 21–24)

amplector, -i, -plexus sum	I embrace
artus, -us (*m.*)	limb
cingo, -ere, cinxi, cinctum	I surround, encircle
complector, -i, -plexus sum	I embrace
Cupido, -inis (*m.*)	Cupid; desire
cupidus, -a, -um	greedy, lustful
digitus, -i (*m.*)	finger
fera, -ae (*f.*)	wild beast
fletus, -us (*m.*)	weeping, tears
flos, floris (*m.*)	flower
formosus, -a, -um	handsome, beautiful
frons, frondis (*f.*)	foliage, leaves, leafy branch
furtivus, -a, -um	secret, secretive
gemma, -ae (*f.*)	gem, precious stone
germana, -ae (*f.*)	sister
germanus, -i (*m.*)	brother
haurio, -ire, hausi, haustum	I drink, drain, consume
immitis, -e	rough, harsh, fierce
improbus, -a, -um	wicked; persistent
invidia, -ae (*f.*)	jealousy; hatred
lacero, -are, -avi, -atum	I tear, mangle
manes, -ium (*m.pl.*)	spirits of the dead; the Underworld
me miserum!	o wretched me! alas for me!
membra, -orum (*n.pl.*)	limbs
metuo, -ere, -ui, -utum	I fear
militia, -ae (*f.*)	military service
naufragus, -i (*m.*)	shipwrecked person
nimius, -a, -um	excessive
nimium	too much, excessively
niteo, -ere	I shine

obstupesco, -ere, -pui (*or* -stip-)	I am dumbstruck, stunned
opacus, -a, -um	dense, thick
opto, -are, -avi, -atum (+ ut)	I choose; I wish for, desire (that)
pingo, -ere, pinxi, pictum	I paint, draw, colour
quare?	why?
rogus, -i (*m.*)	funeral pyre
sono, -are, sonui, sonitum	I make a noise, utter, resound
surgo, -ere, surrexi, surrectum	I rise, rise up
tamquam	just as, like, as though
temerarius, -a, -um	rash, hasty
temere	rashly, hastily
Troianus, -a, -um	Trojan
turbo, -are, -avi, -atum	I throw into confusion, distress
utinam (+ *subjunctive*)	would that . . .! if only . . .!
viduus, -a, -um	bereft, widowed
volucer, -cris, -cre	winged; (*as a noun*) bird

VOCABULARY CHECKLIST 7 (Elegiac and Hexameter Passages 25–28)

abdo, -ere, -didi, -ditum	I hide
anguis, -is (*c.*)	snake
armentum, -i (*n.*)	herd of cattle
avidus, -a, -um	greedy, eager
blandus, -a, -um	flattering, charming, pleasant
cesso, -are, -avi, -atum	I am slow, delay, cease
concito, -are, -avi, -atum	I stir up, arouse
crus, cruris (*n.*)	leg
currus, -us (*m.*)	chariot
cuspis, -idis (*f.*)	spear, javelin
Eurus, -i (*m.*)	East (*or* south-east) wind
excito, -are, -avi, -atum	I stir up, arouse
fax, facis (*f.*)	torch, flame, fire of love
flecto, -ere, flexi, flexum	I bend, turn

fleo, -ere, flevi, fletum	I weep, cry, mourn
fluo, -ere, fluxi, fluxum	I flow
fruor, frui, fructus sum (+ *abl.*)	I enjoy
gemitus, -us (*m.*)	groan
gemo, -ere, gemui, gemitum	I groan, lament
gena, -ae (*f.*)	cheek
grex, gregis (*m.*)	flock, herd
habena, -ae (*f.*)	rein, strap
inanis, -e	empty
late	far and wide
luctor, -ari, -atus sum	I struggle
nix, nivis (*f.*)	snow
os, ossis (*n.*)	bone
pinus, -us (*f.*)	pine tree; ship
placidus, -a, -um	calm, peaceful
praeceps, -cipitis	headlong, rushing
prora, -ae (*f.*)	prow; ship
questus, -us (*m.*)	complaint, lamentation
reluctor, -ari, -atus sum	I struggle against
robur, -oris (*n.*)	oak; strength, manpower
rubeo, -ere	I am red
semen, -inis (*n.*)	seed
simulo, -are, -avi, -atum	I pretend, feign
supplex, -licis	begging, as a suppliant; (*as a noun*) suppliant
tepeo, -ere	I am warm; I feel love
virga, -ae (*f.*)	stick, wand
Zephyrus, -i (*m.*)	West wind

VOCABULARY CHECKLIST 8 (Elegiac and Hexameter Passages 29–32)

ambo, -ae, -a	both
amnis, -is (*m.*)	stream, river
Arctus, -i (*f.*)	the North
auris, -is (*f.*)	ear
Auster, -tri (*m.*)	South wind
caerulus, -a, -um	dark blue, dark coloured
(*or* -eus, -ea, -eum)	
casa, -ae (*f.*)	hut, cottage
clivus, -i (*m.*)	slope, hill
commotus, -a, -um	moved; excited
decus, -oris (*n.*)	honour, glory
dedecus, -oris (*n.*)	disgrace
dono, -are, -avi, -atum	I present, give
ei mihi!	ah me! alas!
exsanguis, -e	bloodless, pale, faint
fallax, -acis	deceitful, deceptive
famulus, -i (*m.*)	slave
famula, -ae (*f.*)	(female) slave
funestus, -a, -um	deadly
genetrix, -tricis (*f.*)	mother
gramen, -inis (*n.*)	grass
inritus/irritus, -a, -um	futile, worthless, ineffectual
iudicium, -ii (*n.*)	judgment, choice
iuro, -are, -avi, -atum	I swear (an oath)
lenis, -e	gentle
lucus, -i (*m.*)	wood, grove
marmor, -oris (*n.*)	marble, statue; sea
marmoreus, -a, -um	of/like marble
mergo, -ere, mersi, mersum	I sink, submerge
merum, -i (*n.*)	wine

Phoebus, -i (*m.*)	Phoebus Apollo (*god of prophecy, poetry and the sun*)
pius, -a, -um	dutiful, pious, devoted
impius, -a, -um	irreligious, impious, undutiful
plango, -ere, planxi, planctum	I strike, beat my breast, mourn
priscus, -a, -um	old, former, ancient
pudor, -oris (*m.*)	modesty, shame
querel(l)a, -ae (*f.*)	complaint, lamentation
remus, -i (*m.*)	oar
udus, -a, -um	wet
vallis, -is (*f.*)	valley
vitium, -ii (*n.*)	vice, fault, sin

VOCABULARY CHECKLIST 9 (Elegiac and Hexameter Passages 33–36)

acutus, -a, -um	sharp
albus, -a, -um	white
amans, -antis (*c.*)	lover
apto, -are, -avi, -atum	I fit, adjust
ardeo, -ere, arsi, arsum	I burn, blaze, am on fire
consuetus, -a, -um	usual, accustomed
cruentus, -a, -um	bloody, blood-stained; cruel
daps, dapis (*f.*)	feast; meat
dimico, -are, -avi, -atum	I fight
egeo, -ere, -ui (+ *gen./abl.*)	I lack, am without
fingo, -ere, finxi, fictum	I make; I invent, fabricate
flavus, -a, -um	yellow, golden; golden-haired
gelu, -us (*n.*)	ice
guttur, -uris (*n.*)	throat
iucundus, -a, -um	pleasant
maternus, -a, -um	of one's mother, maternal
Musa, -ae (*f.*)	Muse (*goddess of inspiration*)
occasus, -us (*m.*)	setting; west

ortus, -us (*m.*)	rising; east
pastor, -oris (*m.*)	shepherd
pecus, -oris (*n.*)/-udis (*f.*)	cattle, herd
piscis, -is (*m.*)	fish
pluvia, -ae (*f.*)	rain
pratum, -i (*n.*)	meadow
profundus, -a, -um	deep
profundum, -i (*n.*)	the deep (sea)
rosa, -ae (*f.*)	rose
sceptrum, -i (*n.*)	sceptre; rule; realm
sedulus, -a, -um	busy, attentive
sidus, -eris (*n.*)	star, constellation
stella, -ae (*f.*)	star
surdus, -a, -um	deaf, unreceptive
uvidus, -a, -um	damp, moist
varius, -a, -um	various, changing, multi-coloured
vates, -is (*c.*)	prophet; poet, bard
ver, veris (*n.*)	spring (*season*)
viator, -oris (*m.*)	traveller

VOCABULARY CHECKLIST 10 (Elegiac and Hexameter Passages 37–40)

acerbus, -a, -um	bitter
adulter, -era	adulterous; (*as noun*) adulterer
aedes, -is (*f.*)	temple; (*plural*) house
aeneus, -a, -um	made of bronze
agrestis, -e	of the countryside
amens, -entis	out of one's mind, mad, frantic
amoenus, -a, -um	pleasant, charming
anima, -ae (*f.*)	soul, spirit, breath, life
antrum, -i (*n.*)	cave
ater, atra, atrum	black, dark

bellus, -a, -um	beautiful, handsome, pretty
bis	twice
cerva, -ae (*f.*)	deer, hind
cervus, -i (*m.*)	stag
cruor, -oris (*m.*)	blood, gore
exanimis, -e	lifeless, dead
fas (*n.*) (*indecl.*)	divine law, right, obligation
for, fari, fatus sum	I speak, say
fors, fortis (*f.*)	chance, luck, fortune
forsitan	perhaps
fremo, -ere, -ui	I roar, murmur, growl
frena, -orum (*n.pl.*)	reins
furtim	secretly, stealthily
grandis, -e	large, great, powerful
Lar, Laris (*pl.* Lares) (*m.*)	household god; home
lepidus, -a, -um	charming, elegant
limen, -inis (*n.*)	entrance, threshold; house
mulceo, -ere, mulsi, mulsum	I soothe, appease
nefas (*n.*) (*indecl.*)	wickedness, crime, wrong
nemus, -oris (*n.*)	wood, forest
nuptiae, -arum (*f.pl.*)	marriage
Orcus, -i (*m.*)	the (god of the) Underworld
perennis, -e	through the year(s), enduring
placo, -are, -avi, -atum	I placate, appease
rupes, -is (*f.*)	rock
sensus, -us (*m.*)	sense, feeling
unguis, -is (*m.*)	nail, claw, talon
vado, -ere (-vasi, -vasum)	I go (*often in compounds*)
vulgus, -i (*n.*)	crowd; common people

Index Locorum

Some of the passages contain omissions from and minor adaptations to the original: the first line alone is given below.

Elegiac Poems

Hexameters

Translation Passages

1 *Metamorphoses* 3.95

2 *Metamorphoses* 3.115

3 *Metamorphoses* 5.648

4 *Metamorphoses* 11.458

5 *Metamorphoses* 1.316

6 *Metamorphoses* 10.23

7 *Metamorphoses* 8.81

8 *Metamorphoses* 14.51

9 *Metamorphoses* 8.201

10 *Metamorphoses* 3.379

11 *Metamorphoses* 13.82

12 *Metamorphoses* 1.525

13 *Metamorphoses* 12.597

14 *Metamorphoses* 11.484

15 *Metamorphoses* 2.270

16 *Metamorphoses* 13.275

17 *Metamorphoses* 4.78

18 *Metamorphoses* 12.146

19 *Metamorphoses* 12.539

20 *Metamorphoses* 6.267

Comprehension Passages

21 *Metamorphoses* 10.567

22 *Metamorphoses* 11.671

23 *Metamorphoses* 11.710

24 *Metamorphoses* 10.247

25 *Metamorphoses* 6.349

26 *Metamorphoses* 2.150

27 *Metamorphoses* 4.571

28 *Metamorphoses* 7.11

29 *Metamorphoses* 10.40

30 *Metamorphoses* 8.689

31 *Metamorphoses* 1.622

32 *Metamorphoses* 11.172

33 *Metamorphoses* 5.438

34 *Metamorphoses* 6.28

35 *Metamorphoses* 4.55

36 *Metamorphoses* 11.100

37 *Metamorphoses* 3.353

38 *Metamorphoses* 13.439

39 *Metamorphoses* 12.553

40 *Metamorphoses* 14.172

CPSIA information can be obtained
at www.ICGtesting.com
Printed in the USA
LVOW10s0121190118
563112LV00007B/374/P